ry beth,
Thank you for
joining me on this
journey Miriam

I Am Because of You

MIRIAM DOBIN

To contact author for speaking engagements:

Iambecauseofyou120@gmail.com

Sales and Distribution:

Amazon.com

ISBN- 13: 978-1514259962

Printed in the U.S.A. by CreateSpace

I didn't come into this world easily. In fact, I never should have been born at all.

When my mother was in her twenties, during World War II, she was a prisoner, her health irreparably ruined in the Auschwitz concentration camp. She was starved and weakened, and her menses ceased, never to return. Though my mother survived the Holocaust, came to America, married, and began to make a new life, she never dreamed that she could have a child. But then, in 1964, ten weeks shy of her forty-eighth birthday, my mother gave birth to me, her miracle baby, her only child.

My memoir, *I Am Because Of You,* is a tale of survival and faith despite terrible odds. My family's journey from near extinction to thriving new generations, from faith to anger and back again, is about ordinary people with the courage to overcome incredible challenges that would permanently derail others. It is about seeing sparks of light in the darkness, about recognizing miracles in this world.

My story traces the journey my parents and my aunt and uncle took to get to America, and details the challenges that arose for all as four Holocaust survivors sought to raise a child in a new country. In suburban New Jersey, I weathered my share of challenges. My mother fell ill when I was a child, and remained in a wheelchair for the rest of her life. I was partially raised by my aunt and uncle, to whom I will forever be grateful, and whom I helped care for until the end of their days.

I am now an Early Childhood Educator with over twenty years of experience. My husband and I raised three children and we recently became the proud grandparents of a baby girl. In the midst of sorrow there was joy, and in the midst of joy, sorrow.

It is important to me and my family that survivors' stories be told. The imperative to remember the toll the Holocaust took on families for generations is equally as important as the imperative to "never forget" what happened during the Holocaust itself. My cousin, the late Hugo Princz, opened up the gates of Germany through continuous pressure by then-President Bill Clinton, to award reparations to all living, surviving victims of the Holocaust--a huge step toward recognition of the atrocities committed during the war. My father and my Aunt Ella recorded their life stories for Steven Spielberg's Shoah Foundation, which documents the history of individual survivors of the Holocaust. These testimonies can be accessed from the University Of Southern California Shoah Foundation Institute. I also recorded an audio version which I have posted on my website, www.iambecauseofyou.net, putting my Aunt Ella's story online for all to hear along with video clips from my visit to the Auschwitz concentration camp and my meeting with Aranka, my family's neighbor. I have included these pieces in conjunction with the memoir.

I hope that you enjoy reading about our journey,

Miriam

From Devorah Hilsenrath

Child Survivor and Noted Lecturer on the Holocaust

I Am Because of You is the autobiography of a daughter of Holocaust survivors. Miriam Dobin offers a sincere, self-analytical memoir of her relationships to everyone dear to her and with whom she has experienced life's encounters. In each instance, Miriam's profound comprehension comes to the sensitive fore. She illuminates with deep affection and awareness the characters in her life as they experience both crisis and joy.

Miriam's story captures those decisions that can be seen as a lesson for all of us in similar situations. As an only child reared by four survivors, Miriam navigated an unusual number of day-to-day encounters requiring important actions.

Through her book *I Am Because of You*, we experience much as we tip-toe through rows and rows of flowers and weeds; life is beautiful and uncertain from moment to moment. We watch as Miriam ultimately reaches that so-called "silver lining" which she has achieved.

Miriam's profound perception of all whom she encounters is vividly and engagingly portrayed in her book. The reader is richly rewarded by reaping the life experiences of Miriam and her family.

DEDICATION

To my parents, of blessed memory
Avrohom Moshe ben Yeshayahu v'Freida
Abraham Moshe, son of Shaya and Fani (née Mermelstein)
Gottesman
August 26, 1907 - October 25, 2003
16th of Elul, 5667 - 29th of Tishrei, 5764
Rivka bas Dovid v'Miriam
Olga, daughter of David and Margit (née Princz) Hecht
June 6, 1916 - June 23, 1988
5th of Sivan, 5676 - 8th of Tammuz, 5748

And to my second set of parents, of blessed memory
Aunt Ella and Uncle Isadore
Yehuda Asher ben Eliyahu v'Sarah
Jakub Isadore, son of Markus Elias and Saly (née Schonbrun) Reich
June 1, 1909 - May 24, 1995
12th of Sivan, 5669 - 24th of Iyar, 5755
Esther bas Dovid v'Miriam
Ella, daughter of David and Margit (née Princz) Hecht
December 20, 1913 - June 2, 2011
21st of Kislev, 5674 - 29th of Iyar, 5771

Hashem divided my childhood and youth between the four of you,
but my love and admiration for how you all raised and nurtured me
will forever remain whole.

Table of Contents

"Now Abraham and Sarah were old, well on in years; the manner of women had ceased to be with Sarah."

Genesis 18:11

"G-d had remembered Sarah as He had said...Sarah conceived and bore a son to Abraham in his old age."

Genesis 21:1, 2

"The Jews constitute but 1% of the human race. It suggests a nebulous dim puff of star dust lost in the blaze of the Milky Way. Properly the Jew ought hardly be heard of; but he is heard of, has always been heard of. His contributions to the world's list of great names are away out of proportion to the weakness of his numbers. He has made a marvellous fight in the world, in all the ages; and has done it with his hands tied behind him. He could be vain of himself, and be excused for it. The Egyptian, the Babylonian, and the Persian rose... the Greek and the Roman followed, and made a vast noise, and they are gone. The Jew saw them all, and is now what he always was, exhibiting no decadence, no infirmities of age, no dulling of his alert mind. All things are mortal but the Jew. What is the secret of his immortality?"

Mark Twain (1835-1910), excerpt from *An Essay Concerning the Jews*

"For you are a holy people to Hashem, your G-d; Hashem, your G-d, has chosen you to be for Him a treasured people above all the peoples that are on the face of the earth. Not because you are more numerous than all the peoples did Hashem desire you and choose you, for you are the fewest of all the peoples."

Deuteronomy 7: 6, 7

PROLOGUE

Summer 1995

"Aunty, one day I'd like to go with a group to visit Auschwitz. It's important to me to see where you and Mommy were." Aunty was visibly upset.

"Don't go there."

"There won't be Nazis there, Aunty."

"It doesn't matter. Don't give them your money," she said.

"Maybe one day I'd like to go to England."

"They were worse than anyone else." Aunty's tone was filled with tension.

In other words, what Aunty was telling me was she didn't want me stepping foot on European soil.

July 2014

As I stood before the graves of my mother, father, aunt and uncle, I cried and asked for their forgiveness. I'm positive they understood why I was doing this and no forgiveness was necessary. I was going to Auschwitz because I needed to see for myself where they spent the worst and most tragic days of their lives and where the majority of my family perished.

WHO AM I?

Forty days before a person is born, a voice from heaven calls out, "So-and-so will marry so-and-so." This is written in the *Talmud*, the Oral Law that was passed down from G-d to Moses and so on down the line to the Jewish people. What isn't discussed is why you are born into the family in which you are born. There are so many types of family units; no two are alike. What happens when situations or tragedies from the past affect your future, and that of your children? How well-adjusted will the children be? In turn, what kind of parents will those children become?

Growing up, I was the center of the world to four people: my mother, father, aunt and uncle. Some people think that as an only child you are privileged. I wasn't spoiled; I didn't get everything I wanted. I never wanted for much because I really had everything I needed. Life isn't perfect. Why was I born into the family that I was? Some years ago, I began to understand why.

My dear parents, of blessed memory, were not youngsters when I was born. They no longer had their parents to lean on for help. They experienced joy, but also much loss in their lives. Luckily they had my mother's older sister, my Aunt Ella, whom I called Aunty, and her husband Uncle Isadore, to lend them a hand when necessary, although they weren't youngsters, either. The fact is, I grew up among old people.

I believe G-d placed me in this family for several reasons, four in particular of which I've tried to accomplish and which have become clearer and more meaningful throughout my lifetime:

- Helping aging parents

- Being a witness to victims of the Holocaust

- Transmitting the religiosity of the family

- Recreating and restarting the family

Looking back over the past forty-nine years, I have learned many lessons and hope that what I took from my own upbringing has been imparted to my children for the good. This book helps me to achieve those responsibilities. It is more than my job, but my opportunity to show appreciation for all that my family has done for me.

Growing up among elderly survivors wasn't easy- not for them living under a shadow of the past, nor for me, knowing all my life that these giants, these people, exemplified survival of the fittest, came back from hell and continued with life. My life was born from their experiences, from their ashes.

We all have a story. You are going to hear the stories of these four people as I tell you my story. This story of heroism, strength, loss, life, and love of family is about my wonderful family of origin, whom I miss deeply. It is about my four parents and the unexpected birth that created a future that so easily might not have been.

MAZAL TOV! IT'S A GIRL

"Congratulations, Mrs. Gottesman! You have a 100 percent perfectly healthy baby girl." My mother, she should rest in peace, frequently told me the story of how she came to give birth to me. Giving birth still carries risk, even in today's age of technology. At my birth, my mother was ten weeks shy of turning forty-eight years old, and to give birth to a healthy child was truly a miracle.

I was born in Maimonides Hospital in Brooklyn, New York, in 1964 and was named Miriam Frances Gottesman. I was given the name Miriam after my grandmother on my mother's side, and Frances after my grandmother on my father's side, whose Yiddish name was Freida. But the story of my birth really began years earlier, when my mother was first a prisoner in the Auschwitz concentration camp in Poland, then transferred to Nuremberg, Germany, and then to Holýšov, Czechoslovakia from June 1944 to May 1945. That horrific time never left my mother, but her unbelievable strength was already evident then and would support her for the rest of her life.

Growing up I knew that my parents were somehow different than my friends' parents. They were old, and they spoke English with a heavy accent. My parents were born and raised in Czechoslovakia, before World War II. Moreover, they were Holocaust survivors. My parents were nine years apart in age. When I was born, Mommy was close to forty-eight years old, and Daddy was fifty-six. I am an only child. I would always joke with them that they were like Avrohom (Abraham) and Sarah in the *Torah*, the Old Testament, because of their ages when they had me. Abraham was one hundred and Sarah was ninety when they had Yitzchak (Isaac), their only child.

We were always a close-knit family. My mother and my aunt Ella, her older sister by two-and-a-half years, were the only two survivors from their family of two parents and six children. By "survivors" I'm referring to those who lived through one of the most horrific tragedies in human history: the Holocaust, the near annihilation of Europe's Jews by the Nazis. My father's family story is even more tragic, if that is possible: of the nine children in his family, five siblings died before the war, and two were murdered in the death camp in Auschwitz, Poland, along with both of my father's parents.

Nine years prior to World War II, my aunt Ella, whom I always referred to affectionately as Aunty, got married to a wonderful man, Uncle Isadore Reich.

Aunty and Uncle both survived the concentration camps and were reunited shortly after the war upon their return to Sečovce, the town where they lived prior to going into hiding in 1942. They unfortunately were unable to have their own children. Uncle would have adopted a child, but Aunty felt that she didn't want to raise someone else's child. The irony was that Aunty and Uncle did share in raising a child, their sister's child, and were wonderful and natural at becoming parents.

My grandparents on my mother's side were David and Margit Hecht. (Her given name was Maria but she was called Margit.) David Hecht was born in 1888, and Margit Hecht (nee Princz) was born in 1892. They married in 1912 and resided in a town called Svalyava, in Czechoslovakia. Their first-born child, my aunt Ella, arrived December 20, 1913. Six weeks later they moved to the town of Abara (Hungarian for Oborin) on the border of Austria-Hungary.

My mother Olga was born on June 6, 1916, and was the second of six children. There were four girls and two boys: Ella, Olga, Ernő, Blanka, Roze, and Zoltan.

Both David and Margit were raised in Orthodox Jewish homes, and when they married they continued this tradition, which meant that the Hecht family observed *Shabbat*, the Sabbath. Another pronunciation for Shabbat is *Shabbos*; I will refer to this holy day as *Shabbos* because that is how I was taught and raised. Every Friday evening, from sundown through Saturday evening until one hour after sundown, no business or labor is allowed to be conducted. It is a day of rest for us and for prayer to G-d. Living life as an Orthodox Jew meant, and still means today, going to *shul*, synagogue, daily for the men, as well as on all the Jewish holidays; keeping a *kosher* home (eating only meat and poultry slaughtered ritually according to Biblical laws, fish that have both fins and scales, and dairy and meat products separately); as well as going to *cheder*, Jewish school, every day. This was the life my grandparents and their children lived in Oborin.

My grandmother wore a *shaitel,* a wig, to cover her hair because according to one interpretation of the Torah, married women must cover their hair. A woman's status changes when she marries – she is beginning a new life. Her hair, which is considered a significant aspect of a woman's beauty, should be seen and enjoyed only by her husband and family. This is a form of modesty. My grandmother, like many Jewish women then and now, adhered to this practice, as I do and as my daughter does.

The language spoken in my grandparents home was Hungarian. At times, they also spoke Yiddish, a combination of Hebrew and German. In their family, education was very important, but since my grandparents didn't have enough money, the girls had to stay at home to help their mother.

Judaism was clearly an integral part of their lives, yet they were also able to integrate into society, have a profession, conduct business, and live a religious life, not unlike today's Orthodox Jews.

My grandfather was a notary public. He also owned a general store, selling home goods on the front porch of their house. My grandmother helped run the store. Even though they were a middle-class family, they had a nanny, who was not Jewish, who would come every morning to help my grandmother get the girls settled and to *daven*, to pray, with them their daily prayers. She had respect for my grandparents and how they were raising their family, and learned much about Judaism.

My grandparents house consisted of a living room, kitchen, and two bedrooms. The boys slept in the kitchen and shared a bed that they closed up in the morning. Two of the sisters slept in another room and shared a bed, and the other two sisters shared a bed in the same room in which their parents slept. It was not the healthiest way to live, as Aunt Ella explained. There was also a barn, where they had a cow, dogs, cats, chickens and geese; once, they even had a turkey. Aunt Ella had to pluck feathers from the geese. Every morning my mother milked the cow, and they would have fresh milk. My mother, it seems, was a strong girl, and this was her job. No one else liked doing it. Aunt Ella helped cook and clean, too.

My grandfather, or *zaidy* in Yiddish, and his two sons went to *shul* in a house right near where they lived, and there was just barely a *minyan*, a quorum, every Shabbos. My grandmother, or *bubby* in Yiddish, would light candles to welcome in the *Shabbos*. The family had a big meal, which always consisted of *cholent*, traditional stew. The men would sing lots of *zemiros*, songs special for *Shabbos*. On *Shabbos* morning, the girls always had cheesecake for breakfast.

The Oborin neighborhood that Mommy and Aunty grew up in was very small. All together there were eight Jewish families who lived there. The rest of the neighbors were non-Jews, but they were very nice to the Jews. All the girls stayed at home to help their mothers, so you would rarely see them. Girls dressed in a simple fashion, usually wearing a plain skirt and a blouse. The houses were also very small, but everyone had a large yard around their home. There was a well on my grandparents' property that they shared with another family, and every day they would draw water from the well.

Aunty occasionally spoke about her maternal grandfather who, she said, hardly ever talked and was thought to have Alzheimer's disease. Her paternal grandfather had a long pipe and always had a *gemara* (Talmud), a *Chumash* (Pentateuch), or a newspaper open. His name was Aleksander. Mommy's and Aunty's paternal grandmother had died from the Spanish influenza. She had been well-liked in the community. Many years later, when Mommy and Aunty were settled in America, somebody came into Aunty's dress shop and asked Aunty if she remembered her. Aunty said that she did remember her, and the other woman said, "Your grandmother was like an angel."

(L to R) Ella, Margit, Rozsi, Ernő, David and Olga

David Hecht, Aunty and Mommy's father and my *zaidy*, had left Czechoslovakia in 1922 to come to the United States to make a better life for his family. The plan was for him to earn enough money to send back home in order to bring his wife and children to the United States. However, not everything goes according to plan. Margit, my *bubby*, was at home with four small children and would have had to carry the burden alone for quite a while, but a few days after he left, David unexpectedly returned. The way Aunty explained, her father realized how difficult all this would be, and was already missing his family.

Aunty would describe the hardships of everyday events that we take for granted. The family lived in a village that didn't have indoor plumbing, so they used an outhouse. While today we often wash our clothes sometimes several times a week, in pre-war Oborin doing laundry required lengthy preparation. Boiling water was poured into a very large tub or pot, and the clothes were left to soak. Then the water had to be changed and the clothes wrung out and hung up to dry. A woman came in to help with the laundry.

Girls didn't go to *cheder* like the boys did. They had a *melamed*, a teacher, come after school to teach them how to read Hebrew in order to know how to *daven* from a *siddur*. Aunty went to a Hungarian public school, but only until eighth grade.

Still, Aunty described her childhood as a happy one. The Hechts were a close-knit family. The girls made their own clothes and even some toys, such as dolls. Aunty was a skilled and creative seamstress. She learned to sew at a young age, and this served her well because it became her profession later in life. She also crocheted and did petit point. To this day, I have a number of the pieces that she embroidered. (My daughter, Rivki, seems to share a love for this as well, because she has made several latchhook designs of her own.)

When Aunty Ella was around twelve years old, she spent the summer with an aunt who resided in the country. The air was cleaner and better for her breathing. Aunty's parents thought she might have asthma, but later in life, a brown spot formed around her collarbone area, and it was determined that she had pleurisy. Pleurisy is an inflammation of the lining of the lungs that leads to sharp chest pain when you take a breath or cough.

My mother and aunt may have been sisters, but they had very different personalities and interests. I loved listening to them tell stories of their childhood in Europe. Aunty would tell me how very social Mommy was. She enjoyed visiting friends and chatting with the neighbors; she liked to dance and to ride her bicycle. Aunty was more introverted. She was a homebody and loved to read. She was a quiet person, but everyone who knew her, loved her. After she came to America, Aunt Ella was active in her synagogue's sisterhood; she was a charitable person and wanted to help others. She received an award from the sisterhood of her *shul* in Perth Amboy, New Jersey, Congregation Shaarey Tefilah, where she *davened* for over forty years.

Aunty was a serious person. She didn't laugh much. She would say that there wasn't much to laugh about. There were times, though, when she would laugh. I remember as a young child asking her once, "Aunty, why is the chicken soup yellow? Do you squeeze the chicken?" Uncle smiled, but Aunty not only laughed, but laughed so hard that tears ran down her face.

One day in 1935, Aunt Ella went into the store where her future husband Isadore worked, and they saw each other for the first time. A *shadchan*, matchmaker, made an arrangement and the next time they met was at a wedding that they were both invited to. Isadore asked her to dance. Aunt Ella liked him very much. She said, "He has kind eyes." They married on August 20, 1935. For the next few years there was happiness and stability.

In 1941, Mommy married Jozsef Strauss, but a few months later in that same year, the Hungarian Nazis disturbed her young married life, taking her husband away for about six weeks to a ZAL (acronym for forced labor camps- Zwangarbeitslager). He then returned home for about one year, only to be taken away again to a ZAL by the Hungarian army and he died in a Russian camp as a Prisoner of War. There was no child from this first marriage. When her husband was taken away she wanted to say goodbye to him, and she was beaten by Hungarian soldiers.

*Olga Gottesman with first
husband, Jozsef Strauss*

Ella and Isadore Reich

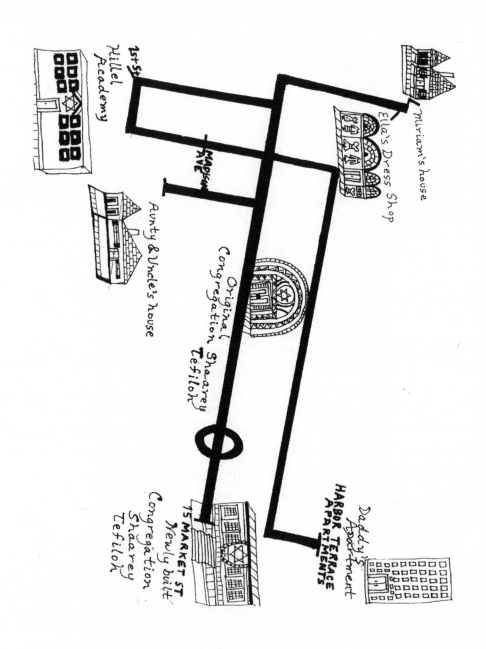

Miriam's life in Perth Amboy, NJ

THE EARLY YEARS

I don't have many recollections of my home in Brooklyn. I remember Brooklyn as very cold and colorless. Aunty told me that one Sunday when we were visiting them in New Jersey, we all drove to Roosevelt Park in Edison. As I approached the lush, green grass, I stopped walking because I didn't know what it was and became frightened by the unfamiliar grass.

My father owned a dry goods store called Morris's General Dry Goods in Brooklyn, on Prospect Place. He sold men's clothing, china, and bicycles. My father employed a couple of young Spanish men. One day after the store was already closed, there was a hold-up. My father suspected that one of his workers had brought someone in to rob the store with him. They pulled a knife on my father, and cut a vein in his neck, and knocked out his teeth. It was a miracle that he didn't bleed to death. I remember little about that day but recall later being held in my uncle's arms, with Aunty standing next to us. We were looking up at my parents, who were standing at the window of the hospital where my father was recuperating. Both my mother and father were smiling down at me. I couldn't understand why I wasn't with them. I remember that my father's face looked very thin and pale. After this horrible experience we left Brooklyn and moved to Perth Amboy, New Jersey.

I was four years old when we moved from Brooklyn to Perth Amboy, New Jersey. My Aunt Ella and Uncle Isadore lived in Perth Amboy and Aunty owned her own dress shop, appropriately called Ella's Dress Shop. My parents bought our home on Maple Street, which was directly across the street from Aunty's business. Perth Amboy was the logical choice because Mommy wanted to live near her older sister, her only remaining sibling.

When we moved to Perth Amboy, I began preschool. Mommy was a stay-at-home-mom so she was able to accompany me to school. I remember the first day of nursery school very clearly. Mommy brought me into this huge classroom. There were many children playing in the kitchen area. The teacher, Mrs. Smith, was a heavy-set woman and not very friendly. My mother was ready to leave, and I began to cry. Clinging to her dress, I begged her, "Mommy, don't leave me!"

This was a whole new experience for me; I had never been in preschool or any playgroup before. This was my first exposure to being with strange adults, as well as children. My mother left and I felt all alone. I observed the children playing, but didn't approach them. I went to a table, sat down, and put my head down over crossed arms. I peeked out and saw Mrs. Smith sitting at her desk, not looking at me. I couldn't understand why this person had seen a new child come into the class and wasn't paying any attention to her at all. I eventually got up and went to explore these new toys, and shyly began to make friends in this new place where my days would begin from now on.

The name of my school was Hillel Academy. It was a *Yeshiva*, a Jewish private school that went from nursery school through eighth grade. It was a large building to which most of the students needed to be bussed from nearby communities. It was over a mile from my house. Mommy didn't drive, so Uncle picked me up in his white Buick and drove me to school every day before going to his job. Daddy didn't drive either. Daddy told me that he had taken the driving test, but failed, and didn't take it again. He didn't really need to drive because he took the train daily to the Lower East Side in New York, where he worked in a men's clothing store similar to the one he had owned in Brooklyn.

Uncle worked for a store called Two Guys in Fords, New Jersey. He was the manager of the fabrics department. Uncle was a very friendly person and everyone liked Izzy, as he was affectionately called. I remember going with Aunty and Uncle on a Sunday to do some shopping there. Some of the employees saw Uncle and greeted him with a friendly word and a smile. He worked there for seventeen years. After he retired, he stayed with Aunty in the dress shop. He always had a calming smile and a positive word to say. In general, he was a quiet man, but when he had a conversation with you, it was always thoughtful, and he watched his words carefully. He was a very caring, kind, and good-hearted individual. He got along well with people. I loved him dearly.

Many years later, Aunty told me that Daddy didn't want to put me in *yeshiva* because it was expensive. Aunty and Uncle said to him, "After what we went through, and you want to put her *there* [public school]?" My aunt and uncle paid the *yeshiva* tuition from nursery school through seventh grade. Aunty and Uncle had lost almost everyone in the war. They had grown up in Orthodox families, had miraculously retained their faith, and would never abandon the beautiful upbringing they loved and cherished. Unfortunately, they weren't blessed with children of their own, but in *Hashem*'s hidden way, they ended up sharing a child with their sister and brother-in-law. Truly I had two sets of parents. I felt very loved and protected. (A bit obsessed-over many a time, but nevertheless, very blessed.) When I went on to eighth grade, leading into *yeshiva* high school, Aunty said to Daddy, "Now, it's your turn to pay the tuition." Daddy did so, gladly!

Each day, when school was over, Uncle would pick me up and bring me home. He kept his car in our backyard while working with Aunty in the store. Mommy was a stay-at-home mom. I would have a snack and then usually go over to Aunty's dress shop and visit with her for a while. I had no siblings, and spending time in her store was a lot of fun. There were rows and rows of dresses to look at. There were so many different colors and textures of material. One of the perks that Aunty offered her customers was free alterations with their purchase. Uncle had a desk that he would sit at and add up the figures at the end of each day. When there weren't customers in the store, he would go in the back room and bring out rectangular cardboard boxes that he put together to pack the dresses in when they were ready to be picked up. The boxes were gray, with a hand-drawn picture of a woman standing in a flowing dress, and the words "Ella's Dress Shop" off to the side. Uncle showed me how to fold the corners of the boxes and fit them together like a puzzle. I was very proud when Uncle carefully packed a dress in one of my boxes and handed it to a customer with a smile.

While I was in the store, Uncle would help me with my homework. He would affectionately call me Miriamku or Miriamkala. He was very patient and explained anything I didn't understand, such as words needing to be translated from Hebrew into English, or certain math concepts. Sometimes Uncle and I would play card games, like Rummy, or board games. I enjoyed spending time with him; he really was like a second father to me.

Mommy and Aunty had a first cousin, Hugo Princz. Their mother and Hugo's father were sister and brother. Hugo had owned different businesses over the years, but at that time, he and his wife, Delores (or as she was lovingly called, Sissy) owned a booth at the local flea market. Among the items they sold was fourteen-carat gold and sterling silver jewelry. They asked Aunty and Uncle if they could display their wares in Aunty's dress shop. They even supplied a display case. I would watch how Aunty or Uncle would show the jewelry when a customer was done purchasing a dress. Some people would buy a necklace to go with their new dress. When I saw a customer eyeing some jewelry, I would go over and play the saleslady, offering to help pick out something pretty. Even Aunty and I bought some of the necklaces.

One day, Aunty had a surprise for me. She handed me a cardboard box and I shook it. Something was rattling around inside. I asked, "What is it?" and Aunty replied, "Open it." I was so excited. I opened it up to find a Dawn doll. I was so happy. It was a beautiful, six-inch doll with long blond hair and a blue halter-top connected to a pleated white skirt. Aunty knew that I would love it, and she was so right!

Aunty did many thoughtful things for me. She was a very talented and skilled seamstress. She would crochet vests, sew dresses, and make costumes for me. She even made clothes for my dolls! Aunty bought me a Barbie doll case, which also served as a closet. It was very cool! I had a Barbie doll and a Stacey doll. They each had a section in the case for a doll to stand in. In the center were drawers for their clothes and shoes, with a bar above for hanging dresses and skirts. My friends and I would spend hours playing with this toy, and I loved all of the skirts and hats that Aunty sewed for my dolls. Once I went with Aunty to New York to the fashion district where she purchased new dresses for the upcoming season. It was exciting to see the showroom with the latest fashions, and to observe the confidence Aunty displayed in her work.

One *Purim* (Jewish holiday in which we celebrate by dressing in costume) I dressed up as Queen Esther. Aunty made me a light green gown with a matching sash that I wore as a crown. There were silver sequins on the bodice of the gown and around the edges of the crown. I must say, I was a beautiful Queen for the Day. Looking back now, I still remember how deeply I appreciated the attention and love that Aunty showered on me.

To this day, I have some of the wonderful objects made for us by Aunty, including a cape and crown for a King Achashverosh costume for *Purim* that Aunty made for my son Dovid when he was three. Later, my son Asher wore it as well. When I began teaching, she made sock puppets that I still use every year in my classroom and the children always love watching the puppets come to life. She also crocheted two afghans that every time I wrap myself in, to this day, I think of her.

At different points in my life, people would ask me if I was lonely growing up without any brothers or sisters. My reply was, "No, how can I miss something I never had?" The truth is, I was often bored. Luckily, I had a creative imagination to keep me occupied. Sometimes, after school, I would stand on the coffee table in my living room and pretend I was on stage, giving a concert. We had a long, horizontal mirror across one wall in our living room that hung over my piano. (I played piano briefly until shortly after Mommy got sick. Then I didn't feel like playing piano anymore.) But I loved to sing. I would hold a pretend microphone and sing--and sometimes scream--my lungs out. Once when I went across the street to visit Uncle, he greeted me at the door and said he had heard my beautiful singing. I felt embarrassed because I didn't realize how loudly I had been singing.

As a young child, I remember how I would step on my father's shoes and he would walk me around holding onto me so that I wouldn't fall. He would call me *ketzele*, kitten, and we would laugh. I needed to entertain myself much of the time when he wasn't home. Mommy spent much of her time in the kitchen or resting and didn't have a lot of energy. There weren't that many kids my age living nearby. However, I did have two friends, Aliza and Cindy, with whom I attended school and who lived within walking distance from Aunty and Uncle's house. Neither of their families was religious, which made spending time with them on *Shabbos* difficult. Aliza's parents were also Holocaust survivors, but were considerably younger than my parents. She was also an only child like me. I remember going over to her house one *Shabbos* for us to spend the day together. Her family was going to the movies and took me along. We saw *The Mad Adventures of Rabbi Jacob*. It was a bit strange, but funny. Then we went out for ice cream. For dinner, we went to McDonald's. I remember that when we sat down in the booth, I sat down hard on the seat and it hurt. My first thought was, "*Hashem* is punishing me" because the hamburger I was about to eat wasn't *kosher*. When they brought me home,

Aliza's mother told Aunty about our day and Aunty was upset. She told her, "But Lilah, the food isn't *kosher*," to which Aliza's mom replied, "But she ate so well." That was the last time I was allowed to go anywhere with them on *Shabbos*.

Cindy's family was American. She had a brother and a sister and a little dog with a loud bark. I didn't like dogs. That's probably because once, when I was walking on the street with Uncle, a big dog that was not on a leash jumped on him, and I became very frightened. Luckily, Uncle wasn't scared and didn't get hurt.

I went to Cindy's house frequently. We would play house and have tuna sandwiches that her mom would make, which I enjoyed. One Sunday afternoon, her family and I sat around their kitchen table and played the board game, Trouble. I laughed so hard I cried. They also took me to the Great Adventure amusement park with them.

I loved my family, but what I missed was going places and experiencing different things. My family worked hard, they were older, and didn't have the wherewithal to run around. So I invented two special friends, Lori and Stacey. They were sisters and lived two houses down from mine. I would talk to Aliza and Cindy about my two imaginary friends. They didn't believe that these so-called friends existed. Aliza and Cindy were both over at my house one day and wanted to meet Stacey and Lori. I said, "Sure," and we walked over to that house. Boy, what a chance I took. We walked onto the porch and I rang the bell. No answer. I rang again, knocked, and called out, 'Lori, Stacey, are you home? It's Miriam."

No answer.

I told Aliza and Cindy, "I guess they're not home." That was the last time that I talked about these imaginary friends!

MOMMY

I don't know enough about Mommy's past. Unfortunately, we weren't together on a daily basis so the simple as well as the more complex conversations couldn't be had. My cousin, Sissy told me a beautiful story of when my mother first met her. When Sissy became engaged to Hugo Princz, Mommy's first cousin, my mother picked her up off the floor and hugged and kissed her. She was so glad to meet her. This lively personality which my mother possessed ties in with what Aunty told me, that Mommy was a very friendly and social person.

As I recently searched through all the family documents, I discovered a letter which described in part my mother's youthful life and how deeply she was affected by the loss of her first husband during the war years. Coming from a large, close-knit, middle class family, she enjoyed a happy childhood and girlhood, an average education, then stayed home, not being forced to have a job. She was socially and athletically an active person, happy and carefree, looking forward to a peaceful good future.

Jozsef Strauss- Reading this man's name in the newly discovered letter was very strange for me, being that this man was not my father. Mommy was over twenty-five years old when she first married which was older in those days. I knew he was tall, but that was about all I knew. This letter revealed that Jozsef Strauss, Mommy's first husband, was nine years older than her. Mommy never spoke of her first marriage. Growing up, I saw she was sad much of the time, but I attributed this to the loss of her family and to her illnesses since the war years. I never realized that some of that sadness came from being torn apart from her first husband, the man she married and had intended to spend her life with. I knew my parents loved one another, but reading in the letter this description of what my mother went through, I began to understand that she never experienced closure of the tragedy that befell her as a young bride. This traumatic loss of her young husband, coupled with the loss of her parents, two brothers and two of her sisters caused so much sadness and "survivor guilt."

As I read this newly found letter in shock, it was difficult to comprehend the strength my mother had to have had to be able to move on with life. She couldn't forget her first husband, who had been literally ripped away from her, yet she was able to move forward, clearly with the help of Aunty and Uncle, remarry and build a new life. My parents tried for years to have a child; they both desperately wanted to rebuild the families they each had lost. I can only assume that Mommy felt this desire to have a child even more so knowing that since Ella and Isadore couldn't conceive, the desire to continue the Hecht/ Gottesman family lineage weighed heavily on her.

Mommy would talk to me about some of her experiences while in Auschwitz. She said there were Jewish guards called *Kapos*, camp police, assigned to oversee the other Jews. Mommy said they were worse than the Nazis because they felt they had to prove that they were brutes to save themselves. Many of them were killed in the end. She explained that, at times, she would open a big mouth to them, and was slapped in the face. These were women!

She described how during one selection while in Auschwitz, her mother and two younger sisters were taken away. She had hoped to be able to get them out, but couldn't succeed and was struck hard on her head when she asked if she couldn't save them. Mommy described in detail what occurred during an *appel*, selection. As the selection line formed, Mommy and Aunty lined up behind their mother and their two sisters. The soldiers called out who should go to the left and who should go to the right. Aunty was told to go to the right, which meant she would be sent to work. My mother, grandmother, and two aunts were chosen for the line on the left. This line was to go to the crematoria. They already knew this from previous *appels*. In all the commotion of people running to the left and to the right my mother took a real chance and ran from the left to the line on the right. Doing this dangerous yet heroic act saved her life! This took place in September 1944, three days after Yom Kippur, the holiest day on the Jewish calendar, the Day of Atonement. She never saw her mother and younger sisters again. Her father and two brothers were separated from the family upon arrival in Auschwitz and all perished later.

While Mommy was in Auschwitz, her menses ended. This was not unusual and had occurred to many of the women there, because the inmates were starved, and the little bits of food that they were given were of no nutritional value. Mommy's menstrual cycle didn't return after the war.

In October 1944, after being in Auschwitz over a period of four months, and experiencing the tragic and horrifying loss of her parents and four of her siblings, Mommy was taken (with Aunty) to the labor camp of Nuremberg in Germany. There she worked with electric bulbs etc... There was little food, bad conditions and she was often beaten.

Mommy went through having injections, finally got her menstruation, had one miscarriage in 1962, and later had a healthy daughter in March 1964. When a woman is able to conceive naturally and give birth without complications, it is a blessing that many may take for granted. How much more so when a woman has great difficulty conceiving naturally. What frustration and sadness she must have felt. It was close to twenty years that she didn't have her menstrual flow, being unable to conceive a child. What incredible joy Mommy must have experienced after giving birth through such a miraculous circumstance.

I have very few memories of doing things with my mother before I was ten because she wasn't physically well much of the time. In 1965, just one year after I was born, she had a tumor removed from her brain. Mommy had long hair and she always wore her hair up in combs to hide the deep depression in her skull. Daddy told me that years earlier while he and Mommy were crossing a busy street in Brooklyn, she suddenly stopped, unable to walk. Daddy had to stop the cars and then somehow got my mother moving again. Another time, Mommy and I were getting out of

Uncle's car when visiting, and while walking, Mommy fell onto the sidewalk. It always seemed to me that she either moved slowly or was sick. Mommy didn't have much energy. I don't recall her doing much other than cooking, shopping, and resting often. I do know that when she was living in New York, she worked as a seamstress for a dress shop called Gerry Price. This was before my father opened his store and my mother worked with him.

Once when I came home from school, Mommy was in bed after having oral surgery in which several teeth had been pulled. Mommy and Daddy both had full dentures. They told me that in Europe, they hadn't had problems with their teeth. After coming to the United States, they felt the air and different kinds of food caused many of their dental problems. Aunty and Uncle had partial dentures, and they felt this had happened for the same reasons. Only many years later did Daddy explain how he really had lost most of his teeth. It is a frightening story to hear of someone knocking out your father's teeth.

I remember when Mommy and I walked together into town to the cinema to see *Bambi*. I cuddled with her during the film, but when Bambi's mother was shot, I put my head down on her lap.

I remember always being a skinny child, so Mommy tried to cook food that I would eat and enjoy. I liked her *Shabbos* cooking: gefilte fish, which is a combination of carp and other minced fish, and chicken soup with noodles. During the week, it was a bit more difficult. Mommy would make spaghetti and meatballs, which I loved! The only problem was that she would sprinkle sugar on top. It was disgusting! I complained that I didn't like it, but I was always told, *"You have to eat it."*

I asked her why she had to put sugar on it and she said, "Because it's good." Maybe for her, but not for me. This must have been similar to the food my parents ate in Europe because Daddy would make noodles for himself and put sour cream and sugar on them, too. One time, when Mommy wasn't looking, I took a napkin, scooped up the pasta, and threw it in the garbage. Mommy looked at my plate and said, "Look, you ate it up so good." I guess I was hungry that evening.

ONE CHILD, TWO HOMES

One afternoon in May 1974, when I was ten years old, Uncle brought me home from school as usual, but I remember entering through the back of the house instead of through the porch in the front, as I usually did. I walked in and saw my mother sitting at the kitchen table with her right arm in a sling, her right leg extended, and her mouth twisted in an odd shape. Aunty was also in the kitchen by the stove. I found this unusual because she was supposed to be in her store. I said, "Mommy, what happened?" She started to cry. What happened next is fuzzy, but I think that Aunty must have taken me outside and across the street. The ambulance was on its way to take Mommy to the hospital. I recall speaking with someone on the sidewalk who said, as the ambulance whisked my mother away, "Don't worry, your mother will be okay."

The telephone was kept on my mother's night table, so I'm assuming that she fell somewhere between her bedroom and the hallway adjacent to the kitchen. How else could she have contacted my aunt? I do vaguely recall being told that Mommy was screaming for help, so perhaps a neighbor heard her, and went to get Aunty, who had a key to our house and was able to let herself in. My mother was a heavy woman. My guess is that Uncle locked the store, came across the street, and then he and Aunty worked very hard to get her onto a chair.

That night, and for the next twelve years of my life, I lived with my Aunt Ella and Uncle Isadore. Thank G-d for them! This actually seemed like the most natural thing to do. We were a very close family, and my going to Aunty and Uncle felt comfortable and safe. I assume that Uncle called my father at work on the Lower East Side of Manhattan to tell him this devastating news. I don't remember who explained to me that my mother had had a stroke. Her right side was paralyzed. She would need to stay in the hospital, where she would receive different therapies to help her get better. She was fifty-eight years old at that time, which isn't old, but after having gone through so much physically and emotionally in her life, coupled with the fact that she was a heavy-set woman, recuperation was difficult.

I went to visit her shortly after she was admitted. Her mouth was still twisted, so she couldn't speak to me. I spoke to her about school. I told her not to be upset and that she would get better. She cried.

Luckily, after about a month, Mommy was doing better. She was receiving speech therapy to improve and bring back her language, physical therapy to walk again, and occupational therapy to regain use of her right arm and hand. Her mouth had "untwisted" and she could speak, but not so clearly; this would improve over time. I would accompany her to physical therapy, and watch while the therapists helped her out of her wheelchair and walked her to the parallel bars to practice walking back and forth. It was difficult to see how slow the progress was. I would try to encourage her by saying, "You can do it, Mommy. Look, you're walking." She would smile, and the therapists would also encourage her. "You see, Olga, what a good daughter you have."

I don't recall how long Mommy was in the hospital, but she was improving and we were allowed to bring her home for holidays. While Aunty was at work, Uncle, Daddy, and I went to the hospital to pick Mommy up. She and I sat in the back seat of the car, where I would cuddle close with her as her left arm draped around my shoulders. When we arrived home and drove into my backyard, the most unbelievably difficult job for my father and uncle would begin. First, Uncle would move the wheelchair to the back door of the car. Then Daddy would climb into the back seat and move Mommy to the edge of the seat, where Uncle would pull her to a standing position. She had to work with them, which was very difficult because she had to have help to turn to sit in the chair. That was step one. Step two was wheeling the chair to the steps. There were four steps to climb to get Mommy up the stairs. Daddy then carried up the chair, she sat down, and Daddy tilted the chair over a small step to get into the kitchen. The whole process literally took *two hours*! I observed all this in silence from start to finish. At one point, when Mommy, Daddy, and Uncle had to stop midway up the steps and all three had to sit down, I ran into my room and started crying and screaming at *Hashem*, "How could you do this to such a good woman? What did she do to deserve this? She didn't go through enough?" Mind you, I couldn't have been older than eleven at this time. As I wiped my tears and came out of my room, I heard my uncle and father say, "*Gloypsi Gut*," thank G-d. Mommy was in the house. I remember running to kiss her. Later, I apologized profusely to *Hashem* for the way that I had spoken to Him.

We all learned from this experience. Daddy had a ramp built in the back. The next time that Mommy came home, life would be much simpler. Taking Mommy out of the car still took about ten minutes, but once she was in the wheelchair, it was up the ramp 1-2-3, over the small step, and *Baruch Hashem*, thank G-d, Mommy was in the house in less than fifteen minutes--a miracle!

Aunty and Uncle lived in a two-family house, which they owned. They lived downstairs and had tenants upstairs. The tenants had a daughter my age, whom I befriended. Aunty and Uncle's house was small, but then again, it had been meant only for the two of them without children, until now. They had a living room/ dining room combination, eat-in kitchen, bathroom, and one bedroom, so I slept on their pull-out sofabed in the living room. Every evening I would open it up before I went to sleep, and every morning I closed it, put the pillows and folded blanket away on a shelf in Aunty and Uncle's bedroom, and got dressed privately in Aunty's room. I also shared their closet, and Uncle moved a bunch of his clothes into the small closet in the living room. All in all, it was a smooth transition, and I was happy living with them. A simple memory that I have of Aunty was how confident she was in the kitchen. She could peel and slice cucumbers so thinly with a knife, I was in awe. Her baked goods were delicious. Whenever she would bake, I wanted to help. Her response was, "Watch and you will learn." I replied, "I've been watching. Now I want to try." Looking back, I felt she always needed to be in control of any situation large or small. I believe this had to do with not only being the oldest daughter and child in her family, but also because her life had been so out of her control so many years earlier.

Life for my father had clearly changed. He was living somewhat like a bachelor again. He had married late in life, at age forty-five. Now he was sixty-six, his wife was in the hospital, and his only child was not living at home with him. What choice was there? Daddy needed to work. He left the house by seven- thirty in the morning and didn't get home until eight o'clock at night. Aunty felt sorry for him. She took it upon herself to also cook for Daddy when she prepared *Shabbos* meals. She made enough food for him to have plenty for dinner every night of the following week. This went on for the next fourteen years while my mother was in the hospital. Even after Mommy died, Aunty was so used to it that she continued cooking for him for the next ten years.

There were times in my young life that I resented my situation. Even though I loved my aunt and uncle deeply, I missed having my mother to come home to and I missed my house. There wasn't much privacy at Aunty and Uncle's house. I always did my homework at the dining room table and Aunty would be cooking in the kitchen in the next room. She would call out, "Miriam, where are you?" I would sometimes laugh and other times feel exasperated while I would answer, "I'm in here, where else could I be; there isn't much place for me to be anywhere else." There were times Aunty would ask me to do things and I just didn't listen because I was angry that I didn't have a normal childhood with young parents who enjoyed doing family things over the weekend and not just sitting home and relaxing. I understood they worked hard all week and needed this quiet time, but for a young girl it was boring. But then Sunday would come and we would go visit Mommy in the hospital. Looking back to my teenage years, I didn't have many friends where I lived and the few that I had were always busy on a Sunday with their families.

Even though I didn't live at home, Daddy or I would call each other every evening when he came home from work. He would often call me *ketzele*, kitten. Sometimes I would just talk to him; other times, Uncle would talk to him, too. This was our routine. It was logical for me to live with Aunty and Uncle. For me, it was like a role reversal. Many kids go to their grandparents for the weekend; I went to my own house for *Shabbos* to be with Daddy.

When I was in the fourth grade, my friends were going on a *Shabbaton*, a weekend retreat organized by the National Conference of Synagogue Youth (N.C.S.Y.), and I went along. N.C.S.Y. is a youth organization mainly geared to Jewish kids in public school, but kids in *yeshiva* also attend. The social interaction at the retreat was very good for me. There were a lot of kids there who were my age. The food was good. There was singing and dancing, and the rabbis gave speeches I actually listened to. Two weeks later, I went on another *Shabbaton*. I enjoyed the peaceful feeling of *Shabbos* and wanted it to be an integral part of my life. I believe when Mommy fell ill, I was searching for something to fill the void in my young life. I was in *yeshiva* and liked what I was learning. Even more than that I felt a strong belief in what I was learning coupled with being brought up in a traditional Jewish lifestyle. All these aspects of faith were what would cause me to become more observant in my adult life.

In my parents' home, the onset of *Shabbos* on Friday night was always strictly kept. No cooking; the food was prepared ahead of time. When Mommy was home, she would light the *Shabbos* candles, which traditionally is done by the woman of the house to welcome in the Sabbath with light. However, if there is no woman in the house the man lights the candles. I was too young to light. I would light one candle after my *bat mitzvah* at age twelve, the age of maturity for a girl according to the *Torah*. Daddy and I ate our *Shabbos* meal with conversation about our week. Daddy would sing his favorite *niggun*, a song, in Hebrew, *"Kol Mekadesh She'vee"* ("All

Who Sanctify the Seventh Day"). His father must have sung this around the *Shabbos* table when he was a boy growing up in Europe. It was at that point, after my first *Shabbos* home from the previous weeks' *Shabbaton*, that I got up from my seat and went to sit on his lap. I said, "Daddy, this is the way I want us to be." He started crying.

The next day, Saturday, was *Shabbos*. My father called his boss, who was also a Holocaust survivor, and said, "I'm not coming in to work on *Shabbos* anymore. My daughter doesn't want me to."

It seems that his boss understood. The generation of Holocaust survivors was an unusually strong generation in mind and spirit. They should never be judged, just as people shouldn't judge others, in general. After what they had gone through, there were many who grew up religious, but rebelled and were never religious again. Those who hadn't been religious, became so. And others who grew up with religion stayed that way, and their convictions became stronger. My parents, aunt, and uncle had all come from strictly Orthodox homes. They felt, however, that to put bread on their table, they had to work on *Shabbos*. It was not what they wanted, but they felt they had no choice. Many survivors felt the same way. There were others who wouldn't desecrate the *Shabbos*, and had trouble finding work or were fired from their jobs because they refused to work on Saturday. In those days, you couldn't fight religious discrimination and win.

My father started attending *shul* early every *Shabbos*. (I went later. First, I had to have my favorite *Shabbos* breakfast of pineapple cheesecake from Parnes bakery, with a cold glass of milk.) Unfortunately, my father had a difficult time keeping strictly *kosher*.

With meat, fish, and poultry, there was never a question that it would have to be kosher, but with dairy products, he wasn't as strict. I was very influenced by N.C.S.Y. and often went on *shabbatons*. I had been in *yeshiva* since early childhood. I was becoming more observant, and Daddy and I often had clashes about his level of observance. I believe he had conflicting feelings within himself about religion. After having gone through so much and lost so much, he was angry for a long time. From speaking with other survivors, as well as their children, I learned that this was not uncommon. My cousin told me about a well-known rabbi who survived the Holocaust. He was angry with *Hashem* for a long time and turned his back on *yiddishkeit* (living the life of a Torah-observant Jew). Eventually, he returned to a Torah-observant way of life, as did my father.

In Perth Amboy there weren't *kosher* restaurants. It was rare to be able to eat out because it was uncommon to find a *kosher* eatery in New Jersey. However, New York's Jewish population was strong and had *kosher* businesses. Once Daddy brought home a bag of pastries. I looked inside and they didn't look like the baked goods from Parnes. I asked where it was from, and Daddy got upset. I started crying and asked him why he was bringing things home that weren't *kosher*. I was terribly upset. I felt like running away. I had never done this before, but I had to leave the house. Aunty and Uncle lived about six blocks away. I had made the walk with them many times, so I knew the way. As I walked, I kept looking around and behind me to make sure that no one was following me. I was scared. I arrived at Aunty's and Uncle's and started crying. They were surprised that I was alone. I told them what had happened.

Uncle called Daddy after *Shabbos* and said in an exasperated tone, "You have one kid, why can't you do this for her?"

"Because I don't want to," he replied. It seems Daddy wouldn't or couldn't put his anger towards G-d fully behind him, and even though I loved my father dearly, this would be a source of friction between us for many years to come.

Since Mommy was now improving, the hospital discharged her, and we brought her home. I moved back home, temporarily, because Mommy was home and Daddy had hired a nurse to help her during the day and to cook the meals. Daddy had installed wooden bars on the walls in the hallway so that Mommy could walk around the house with greater ease. She still moved extremely slowly, but it was good to have her home. It was difficult to maneuver the wheelchair through the narrow hallway. We had to remove the bathroom door to get the wheelchair in. For privacy, Daddy bought a shower rod and we hung a long towel from it.

Mommy was home for about three months. One day, when she was in the bathroom, she stood up on her own and fell. After that, she had to go back to the hospital. I thought she had lost her balance, but a second stroke must have occurred because we could see that she had suffered a setback. I must have been about fourteen or fifteen years old. Mommy didn't come home as often anymore, but when she did I cherished that time.

Daddy was shorter than average and slender, a spry gentleman full of energy, with a sharp glint in his blue eyes. He was five feet tall and Mommy was five feet four. When he asked her to marry him, he said, "Would you consider marrying a short fellow like me?" They laughed whenever they related this story. Daddy was now in his early seventies, and got tired easily from taking care of Mommy. I was a young teenager, but stronger than I realized. When Mommy came home for holidays or special occasions, I would take care of her. The three of us ate in our large kitchen like we used to many years earlier, except now Mommy sat in her wheelchair, and after dinner, I would clean up. Mommy would take a napkin in her left hand to help me crumb the table. The wooden bars were still along the walls, and I would play on them as if I were a ballerina, or push up on them and try to walk across with my feet dangling, to strengthen my arms. Mommy didn't use them anymore because we were afraid that she might fall again. I would wheel her to the bathroom, help her get up, and then turn her around so that she could sit on the toilet. Then I would sit in her chair and talk to her. Somehow, the conversation would always come around to the time she had spent in the concentration camps. It always haunted her.

She told me that people were assigned different jobs: hers was to give out potatoes. She recounted how poorly she was treated by the *Kapos*. How her mother and two of her sisters had been selected to go to the line on the left which meant death. How she too was sent to the left, but during all the commotion that ensued-- with women going right, left, right, left--she ran from the line on the left to the one on the right. She took a tremendous risk and saved her own life! This was a miracle.

Afterwards, Mommy would wash her hands and rinse her teeth, and I would brush her hair, always noticing the deep indentation in her scalp. I would wheel her to bed and help her in. I would undress her and put her nightgown on her. When I put her in bed, I would make sure that she was far enough away from the edge so she wouldn't fall out. We placed chairs against the bed as a guard rail. But the real reason I moved her further from the edge was so that, after Mommy was in bed and everything was in order, I could go cuddle next to her. I missed her so much, and this was our special time to talk and be like a mother and a daughter should be. In the morning, I would sit her up, and help her into the wheelchair, take her to the bathroom, and afterwards help her wash herself. Then we would have breakfast together in the kitchen. Over the years, different people have said, "Miriam, that must have been such a burden for you." But it wasn't a burden. She was my mother, and it was an honor to take care of her.

When I was fourteen and attending a *shabbaton*, two boys walking by asked how old I was. When I said that I was fourteen, they couldn't believe it. I guess I looked older, probably because of the way I dressed. Aunty bought me suits and dresses for *Shabbos*, and I wore low heels. I also acted and behaved older than my age. My experiences in life had matured me at a young age. That's probably part of the reason I chose to be an early childhood educator; I didn't have a regular childhood.

Each day when I got home from school, I would go to Aunty's shop, and at four o'clock, Mommy would call us from the pay phone in the hospital. Aunty, Uncle, and I would spend every Sunday afternoon visiting Mommy in the hospital (Daddy worked on Sundays). When spring and summer arrived, we would bring snacks or lunch and take Mommy outside to enjoy the weather. Although she was cooped up in the hospital, she always had the nurses dress her daily with dignity. On Sundays, she would wear pretty dresses or slacks with a nice blouse for our visit. Mommy would fix her own hair nicely with combs. She managed to do this using her left hand, and she also would always apply lipstick. It was wonderful that she took the high road, and didn't resign herself to a defeatist attitude. She knew that there was a purpose to her life--her family.

Mommy continued to receive therapy a few times per week. During occupational therapy, she would make beautiful trivets. They would supply a round or rectangular cork base with a metal handle and thin metal rods to support the bottom, and for the surface she had a selection of colorful tiles to choose from. Some were smooth, while others had a rough texture. She was very creative in her layout, and you could see that she gave her designs much thought.

To this day, while cooking and serving dinner or during *Shabbos* meals, I use these trivets that my mother made for us with love. In fact, when we have company, I receive many compliments on the trivets and proudly say, "My mother made them." Aunty also had some, and later on we gave some away to our cousins and my mother in law. Mommy even created and designed two end tables. One had a pattern of small square tiles and the other had a marbled effect. Daddy used one as a lamp table, and the other I used at Aunty's for all my schoolbooks and supplies. I still have these tables. I also gave my daughter Rivki a couple of trivets as a gift from her *bubby* when she was setting up her new home as a young bride.

TRADITIONS

When I was fifteen, Aunty told me that the doctors had found cancer in Mommy's left breast, and that they would have to remove the breast completely--a mastectomy. I was young and didn't fully understand the ramifications. I remember seeing Mommy when she came home and I would dress her. To me, the line of stitches looked like they had butchered her, but in reality, it was a thick line of scar tissue. Mommy was an amazing woman. Of course she would cry, and often would say, "*Ribono Shel Olam*, Master of the Universe-- why?" Or she would say in her native Hungarian, "*Istenem, istenem*, G-d, G-d." But she always would smile for me and be like a mother should be when we were together, asking me questions and telling me how to do things. Even when I was an adult and a new mother myself, her motherly words meant the world to me.

I was in tenth grade at the time. We were learning different commentaries on *Sefer Bereishis*, Genesis, the first of the five books of the *Torah*, and came to the part where Yitzchak (Isaac), Abraham's son, was old and blind and giving his blessing to his son, Yaakov (Jacob). I don't know exactly what it was about this particular portion in this chapter, but after class I asked my teacher, Mrs. Stern, if I could speak with her. I liked her and she was a lovely person. I told her briefly about my mother and that I was angry with *Hashem*. I started crying. I told her how years before I had screamed at *Hashem* for what He had done to her. She said the most amazing thing to me: "*Hashem* understands that you're angry with Him. You love your mother. He's not angry with you." I had such remorse for what I had done, but she explained to me that my emotions were human, that *Hashem* made us, and He understands.

When I was sixteen years old, Daddy either heard from someone or read in the Yiddish newspapers that the Skver *Rebbe* was going to be in the Borough Park section of Brooklyn, New York. (The term *Skver* comes from a town in Ukraine, and refers to a branch of *Chassidim* that originated there in the nineteenth century by Rabbi Twerski. This sect of Chassidim was reestablished in Brooklyn after the war by a descendant of his.) Even though my father was born and raised in Czechoslovakia, and his family descended from *Belzer chassidim*, the fact that a *rebbe* was going to be close by was enough for him to say, "The Skver *Rebbe* is going to be in Brooklyn on Sunday. Let's go get a *brucha* [a blessing] for Mommy." Daddy's pronunciation of certain Hebrew words was a reflection of how he was taught by the Rabbis in Europe. In the United States we say *bracha*, but they both mean blessing. The *Rebbe* was coming and that was what mattered. Certain concepts, ideas and customs had been embedded in him from childhood, regardless of which community a *rebbe* came from.

Sunday came, and we took a train to Penn Station in New York and a subway to Brooklyn. We came to the house where the *Rebbe* would be appearing. We walked into a large living room filled with long-bearded men--many *chassidim*. There were no women. Oh! The women were in the kitchen. Daddy stayed with the men, and I sat in the kitchen with a number of other women. I sat down next to an older woman and began to make small talk. "Where are you from?" she asked.

I told her about my hometown of Perth Amboy. There were two Orthodox *shuls* and one conservative one. There were no *kosher* butchers, so we had to travel thirty minutes away to purchase our meat. There was one *Yeshiva* day school. It was an older community, and I was the youngest person in my *shul*. She listened intently, and remarked that she gave me a lot of credit for living there because she wouldn't be able to do it. I found this an interesting response. It clearly showed that people get used to their comfort zone, and change is difficult but often necessary. I had questions for her also.

"On the street, I noticed many times that the women walk in back of the men. Why?"

She said because it was more modest. I wanted to know why boys and girls didn't speak to each other. She explained that from a young age, boys are taught not to look at girls, to avert their eyes from looking at a woman. Later, when they are ready to start dating for marriage, they can start to look. The girls are told they can start wearing make-up. She said many boys have a difficult time with this because all their lives they had been taught one way, and now the reverse was happening.

After literally three hours of waiting, my father came to get me. The *Rebbe* was ready to meet us. I smiled and thanked the woman I had sat next to for the conversation and for answering my questions, and wished her well. Daddy and I came before the *Rebbe*, and I thought my father would speak. I believe that he said something in Yiddish, "*Mein tochter,* [my daughter]" and then the *Rebbe* looked at me. I took a step back and stood next to my father. I was surprised. I didn't know if I, a girl, should speak to him, but he waited patiently. I told him about my sick mother and he listened intently. He gave a *bracha* for a *refuah shlaima*, a quick and speedy recovery. I don't recall why I stepped back when meeting the

Rebbe. Perhaps because I had just assumed that a man of his stature wouldn't address a woman. In religious circles, it's usual for men to speak with men and women to speak with women. I felt a greater respect for the *Rebbe* because it seems that whomever he spoke to, he gave his full attention, regardless if it was a man or a woman. I received both an education and a blessing that afternoon.

One Sunday each month was meat shopping day. Aunty, Uncle and I would go to Linden, New Jersey, which had the closest *kosher* meat market to our house. It was always crowded. We bought Empire chickens. We also bought lamb chops--that was a real treat. I remember that they had a new item in the meat cases: kosher sausage. It didn't look very appetizing, but we figured we'd try it. It wasn't anything special. We also bought several packages of beef. There was a large sign overhead that read, *ALL MEAT NOT SOAKED OR SALTED*. This meant the meat was slaughtered ritually, according to *Torah* law, but still needed to be *koshered*. A *kosher* animal must possess two qualities: it must chew its cud and have split hooves. *Kosher* meat--cow, bull, lamb, goat, venison, bison-- must be soaked and salted.

When we got home, the interesting and fun part began. Aunty, Uncle, and I unpacked and put away everything except for the meat. Aunty would put several buckets in a row out on the kitchen floor, filled the buckets with water, and place the meat in them to soak. After about thirty minutes, she emptied the buckets and refilled them with water to soak the meat for another thirty minutes. Then she emptied the buckets. The next step was salting the meat. Aunty would place wire racks on top of the buckets and put the individual pieces of meat on the racks. She picked up a piece of meat, and explained to me that you have to salt all six sides of the meat: top, bottom and all four sides. She let me help her and watched that I was doing it correctly. Then she would place it back on the racks for all the blood to drain out of the beef. According to *Halacha*, Jewish law, *Hashem* says in the *Torah* that a Jew is not permitted to eat blood because blood is life. It even goes so far as to say that if you get a cut you're not allowed to suck it. After this process, we would rinse the meat well and store it away. This all took much of the afternoon, but I enjoyed spending time learning from Aunty, and it was very interesting to see this side of her, a part of her that she had brought from her childhood.

When one is keeping a strictly *kosher* home, meat and dairy items may get mixed up in the kitchen, however unintentionally. Aunty had installed a double sink to keep dairy and meat dishes and utensils separate. One time, we found a dairy utensil in the meat sink. When this happens to me in my own home, I call the rabbi to ask what to do. Aunty would take that piece of silverware and stick it deep in the soil for three days. Then it was *kosher* again. I don't understand why, but this is what they did in Europe. When Passover time came, they needed to *kosher* the glasses and any glass objects that were used to hold food. Aunty would fill a large tub of water, immerse the glassware, and leave it there for twenty-four hours. She would change the water every twenty-four hours for three days. When I asked why she was doing this, she would say, "This is what we did at home."

Traditions continued no matter where they lived.

SUMMER TIME MEMORIES

Every summer of my childhood I went to the YMHA day camp in Roosevelt Park in Edison, New Jersey. I remember that one day was dress-up day with a theme. Aunty made me a great Native American costume. It was an off-white dress with embroidery in the center. A photographer from a newspaper came by, and I got my picture in the paper.

After I turned eleven, I spent a month that summer at Massad Aleph, a sleepaway camp in the Pocono Mountains in Tannersville, Pennsylvania. It was the first time I had slept away from home, and it was quite an adjustment. I knew a couple of kids, but I was lonely and homesick for my family. There were plenty of activities to keep me occupied and keep my mind off Mommy. I remember once receiving a care package from Aunty and Uncle. It was a large box of assorted cookies! Some were solid in color, others had a checkerboard design, and some were rainbow. I was so excited. I shared some with my bunkmates. When visiting day arrived, I greeted Daddy, Aunty and Uncle and showed them around the camp. They saw I was managing fine and taking care of myself. When visiting day was over, I began crying. I wanted to go home, but Aunty reminded me that it was only two more weeks, and so I stuck it out. Surprisingly, I went back for two more half-summers. Most of my bunkmates went back, too, and I got over my homesickness.

When I was fifteen, my first job was working as a counselor in a bungalow colony in the Catskill Mountains in upstate New York. Many Jewish families either owned or rented bungalows in an area in the Catskill Mountains every summer to escape the heat of the city. Anyone could do this, but from my experience, it's mainly Jewish families who cling to this annual experience in the Catskill bungalows. Each family has its own bungalow, and the children have a day camp in a separate section of the colony. The fathers come up to spend *Shabbos* with their families, and return to their usual homes and jobs during the week. There are many such colonies throughout the area, and that part of the region comes to life from the end of June through the hot days of August.

At camp in the bungalow colony, I was given the youngest age group, the two year-olds. That was an eye opener, especially because as an only child I had had little experience with such young children. They were very cute, and I learned how to play with them and engage them in fun activities. That summer was a great learning experience for me.

When I was sixteen and in tenth grade, I had many teachers, as well as many rabbis who filled our long days with new and interesting subjects. One of the rabbis ran the day camp every summer in a bungalow colony in the Catskill Mountains where he and his family also rented a bungalow. He was looking for counselors for the different age groups for his day camp. Three other girls and I had expressed interest, and thus we had summer jobs. This was my second job, and I was paid $250 for the full summer. Every day we planned a different schedule with numerous activities such as arts and crafts, a variety of ball games, circle games, swimming, lunch, and snacks. I was in charge of the five-and-six-year-olds. What a contrast from the group I had had the previous summer.

The rabbi hired two additional girls from an all-girls' school like mine in Brooklyn. They were very nice, but somehow different from the four of us. We were all religious, but dressed differently. We wore short sleeves while the Brooklyn girls wore sleeves below their elbows. We kept one button open at the collar, and they wore the top button closed. We wore skirts below our knees, and bobby socks; they wore longer skirts and knee-high socks or hosiery. We talked about boys, they didn't. The differences were noticeable to them, as well. They kept to themselves much of the time. I found it so interesting that we came from communities and schools with similar philosophies, yet we were worlds apart. I chose to believe that these superficial differences didn't matter. We were all Jews and we should all get along. I made it my business to befriend them, and I could see they appreciated it.

As counselors, our days off were *Shabbos* and Sunday. We decided to go into Woodbourne, which was a town comprised of a pizza and ice cream store with a large game room in the back, a bakery, a delicatessen, and a knish shop. The town was two blocks long and was a popular gathering place for the Jewish bungalow colony kids in the summer. My three friends and I were getting ready to go, and we asked the Brooklyn girls if they wanted to come along. They actually looked scared and nervous at such a prospect. They said that if they got caught or seen they would be kicked out of school. I had never heard of such a thing. They explained that this was a rule enforced by all the Jewish girls' and boys' schools in Brooklyn, as Woodburne wasn't an acceptable scene for boys and girls to come together and socialize.

One day, Daddy came up to visit me in the bungalow colony. I think he was surprised at how religious the people were, yet their behavior and dress was similar to the way in which he had grown up. There were some Chassidic families, but mostly just Orthodox Jews. I introduced him to the other counselors and to some of the families with whom I had become friendly. One young mother couldn't have been more than ten years older than me and was very sweet to my father. She had one of her children in tow and I introduced her to my father. He said, "How do you do," bowing his head slightly as he did when he greeted someone. Always the gentleman.

She asked, "Would you like a cookie?"

Daddy started to reply, "No, thank you," but she stuffed the cookie in his mouth and said, "Oh come on, have one."

Daddy laughed and thanked her. I think that in many ways, as he looked around and saw the direction my life was going in, he couldn't get over how, as Jews, we were able to rebuild after the destructive events of the Holocaust, and move forward and live religious lives. He seemed proud of how I was growing up.

In the summer of 1983, when I was nineteen, my father and I flew out to Salt Lake City, Utah, to attend the *bat mitzvah* celebration of my cousin Roni, whose mother, Nomi, is my first cousin. Nomi's father, my uncle Arieh, was my father's sole surviving brother. Nomi and her husband Laury have three children: Roni (named after Nomi's mother, Reny), Gabi (Gabriel), and Adina. Arieh had an apartment not far from them. Arieh had suffered a stroke years earlier, and recovered mentally but not fully physically. He walked with a cane.

Daddy called his brother Leiby because that's how he was referred to by his family. (His full name was Arieh Leib.) My father, Avrohom Moshe, was called Avrohom Moishku. These are pet names. The last time Daddy had seen his brother was in 1976. When my father saw his brother for the first time in seven years, they just looked at each other awkwardly.

I said, "Daddy, he's your brother. Go give him a hug." He did. They were inseparable for the rest of the day, as well as for the upcoming *simcha*, celebration.

That *Shabbos* afternoon, after a celebratory luncheon for Roni with family and friends, there was a large number of children between the ages of four and nine years old playing together. They were a bit loud and rambunctious, so I gathered them together and asked them to form a big circle. We started singing *Shabbat* songs, as well as common children's songs such as, "Row, Row, Row Your Boat," and " Frère Jacques," among others. We also played circle games. This went on for about an hour. Later, Daddy told me that Nomi said to him, while they were both observing this with smiles on their faces, "Uncle Morris, look at your daughter."

Looking back on my early years, I now know what interested me in becoming an early childhood educator. I still recall my first day of nursery; the teacher ignored a new child who was clinging to her mother not to leave. The teacher just sat behind her desk and showed a lack of sensitivity for this young, scared child. Firstly, why was a teacher who was working with this age group sitting behind a desk? She should have been walking around to the different areas where the children were playing and observing what they were doing or participating in some of their play. Secondly, there should not have been a teacher's desk in the room. And why were there thick wooden tables and thick wooden chairs in this room? At least they should have been spread around the room so as not to appear as if soldiers were sitting down to eat in a mess hall.

Daddy was proud of me. I was nineteen years old. I think I knew by then that I wanted to be a teacher and work with young children.

(L to R) Back: Laury Loeb, Hershey and Magda Gottesman

Middle: Morris Gottesman, Miriam (Gottesman) Dobin, Nomi (Gottesman) Loeb

Seated: Arieh Leib Gottesman

HE'S NOT FOR YOU

Earlier in the summer of 1983, three of the four girls from the previous summer went away to a different bungalow colony. There were three new counselors, so I got a new roommate. She was from the Borough Park section in Brooklyn and was Chassidic. Her name was Yetta, but liked being called Yettie. She was friendly, but at the same time a bit aloof. We respected each other's privacy and became friends. We kept in touch over the next several years. I was invited to her wedding when she was nineteen and she came to my wedding when I was twenty-one. (I was three days shy of my twenty-second birthday.) She even let me borrow her crown for my headpiece.

After the summer Yettie and I spoke from time to time. She didn't go to college, which is not unusual in Chassidic circles, and worked in an office as a receptionist. She wanted to fix me up with a religious boy who was a cousin of her employer. At the time, I was around nineteen and attending Stern College for Women in New York City, the sister school of Yeshiva University in the city's Washington Heights neighborhood. The boy called and we set up a date to go out. I was surprised at how Yettie defined "religious." He wanted to go out to eat but was running late, and most of the restaurants were already closed. We went by taxi to one that he seemed to know. The problem was that it wasn't *kosher*! That was my first shock. When we walked into the restaurant, he removed his *yarmulke* (skull cap)--second shock. We were seated, and he asked what I would like. I said I had already eaten something, and just had water (I had eaten very little, but knew that I could eat more when I returned to the dorm). He ordered a salad. He told me about his day at work, and I told him about school. Then he proceeded to tell me about a relationship of his that just ended. I just kept thinking, "What was Yettie thinking, fixing me up with this guy!"

Afterward he brought me back to the lobby of the college dorm. He said he had had a nice time and asked for a kiss goodnight! Third shock.

I said, "No."

The next day when I spoke to Yettie, she said, "Miriam, I had no idea you were so religious."

It seemed to her that because I wasn't of her background, it appeared I wasn't so religious. From this experience, Yettie learned not to "judge a book by its cover."

It was 1984. Daddy was seventy-six years old and I was twenty. He wanted to see me settled. He still worked full time at the same clothing store on the Lower East Side. At this point, I had dated three boys. One day, a tall young man walked into the store. My father called me at school that evening and told me that he had met this boy in the store that day, that he went to Yeshiva University and would be calling me that evening.

I felt my eyes widen in disbelief; "Daddy, how could you do this to me? You don't even know this boy!"

He said, "What? He was wearing a *yarmulke*."

Oy, Daddy.

I asked how this had happened. He said that he had told him that he had a daughter who goes to Stern College and asked if he would be interested in meeting her. The boy asked to see a picture of me, then agreed and took my phone number.

I told Daddy, "I guess I don't have a choice, but never do this to me again!"

The boy and I went out a couple of evenings later. I suppose he had liked my picture because when I came down from my room to meet him, he greeted me with a beautiful rose, but he wasn't as handsome. I went to put the flower in water, returned, and then we walked to dinner. Conversation was slow and boring. After dinner, he brought me back to the dorm, I thanked him, and that was that. Or so I thought. Two years later, after I was married, we had company over for *Shabbos* lunch. I had invited a single girlfriend, as well as a young couple that we had become friendly with. They brought along two single guys who were their houseguests and we all ate together in my apartment. You can imagine the shock on my face when in walked the same guy I had dated two years earlier!

Daddy had a cousin who lived in Brooklyn. He told me that she knew of this twenty-five-year-old man who was religious, had values similar to mine, and whose parents were also Holocaust survivors. He was working, looking to get married, and wanted to settle down.

I didn't know this cousin, and more importantly, she didn't know me, but Daddy was trying to help. This time, he at least spoke to me about the guy first. His name was Sam. He was short, and had a thick shock of black hair and a moustache. When we met, he was wearing a jacket, slacks, and a button-down shirt. He was kind of plain looking. I don't remember our first date, but for our second date we went to the Bronx Zoo. During the safari ride through the African jungle, we noticed "lovebirds" in the wild. Sam commented, "Just like us."

I didn't look at him. I thought, "Enough."

After our second date I still hadn't told him about Mommy, but assumed he knew about her through Daddy's cousin. He took me back to Aunty's house and asked me out again before we got out of the car. I felt put on the spot and said yes, even though I really didn't want to go out with him again. When we got inside, Sam started talking with Uncle about men's clothes, and I thought that the conversation sounded like one between old men. I went into the kitchen where Aunty was cooking and asked her what she thought of him. She stared at the pot and said, "He's not for you."

I agreed but asked, "Why do you say that?"

She said, "Because he comes from Holocaust survivors and you need someone more fun."

What a truly insightful woman she was. She understood first-hand the trauma of living through that nightmare and the burdens that could befall survivors' children.

It was now September and I had just started my junior year at Stern College. My third date with Sam was set for the following week, after the holidays. We went out to eat, and I figured I should be fair and give it one more chance. When I asked about what his days were like, Sam said, "I get up, *daven*, go to work, and go home. That's it." He seemed like a pleasant guy, but not interesting enough for me. I was very quiet for the rest of the date. When he dropped me off at the dorm, there was a young family with a baby and small children getting out of a car. Sam looked at them with a smile on his face and I felt really bad, but that would not be us. We said goodnight. I knew he was hurt, but he had gotten the message, and I didn't hear from him again.

I had a good friend in one of my Judaic studies classes. Annie was dating a medical student and they were serious about one another. At that point, I wasn't seeing anyone. That summer I received a letter from her telling me the wonderful news that she had gotten engaged. I remember telling Aunty, "I'm happy for her, but when is it going to be my turn?"

When you go to an all-girls' school and see a lot of girls getting engaged, you try not to feel it. But at times you feel the pressure that you'll be graduating college soon, and still aren't either engaged or married. It's more difficult to meet people when you're out of school.

In August 1984, Aunty and Uncle surprised me with a vacation to Grossinger's, a popular hotel where meeting people my age was certain. I was so excited and touched by their sensitivity to my feelings. Every summer before this we had gone to the Catskills for a ten-day vacation at different hotels. For me, it could get boring because there weren't many young people at those hotels. At Grossinger's, I met a boy, we chatted for a while, and then he said the same thing to me that another boy had said to me: "You're not the dating kind, you're the marrying kind." I took this as a compliment.

In 1983 I had moved into a new dorm suite for five girls--two in one room, three in the other, plus a kitchen and a bathroom. My roommates and I all got along well, so the following year we decided to room together again. I was beginning my junior year. The Jewish holidays usually begin in September, last three weeks, and include the High Holy Days of *Rosh Hashana*, the Jewish New Year and *Yom Kippur*, the Day of Atonement. *Sukkot* is five days later and lasts for seven days. We are commanded by *Hashem* in the *Torah* to build a *sukkah*, which resembles a hut. Traditionally, it is made of wood, but it can also be made of more modern materials like plexiglass or cloth. We eat all our meals in it, and some people even sleep in a *sukkah*. It's to remind us of how the Jews traveled through the wilderness for forty years, from the time they were freed from Egyptian bondage until they entered the land of Israel.

In 1984, one of my roommates, Sarah, invited me and our other roommate to her house for the holiday of *Simchat Torah*. These are the last two days which concludes the series of holidays which began with *Rosh Hashana*. This is the time of year when we finish reading the last weekly portion in the *Torah* and then start reading from the beginning again. It takes one full year to read the *Torah* from start to finish. It's a very festive time of year.

I knew that Sarah had a brother who had recently gotten married. My roommate, Leah, and I arrived at Sarah's house that Wednesday afternoon a few hours before the holiday began. We were sitting in the kitchen talking with her mother when Sarah's two brothers walked in.

I whispered to Leah, "Which is the married one?"

"The one with the beard," she replied.

"Oh, good," I thought to myself.

Later, I asked Sarah if her other brother, Yaakov, had a girlfriend and she said, "Why? You're interested?"

I said, "Yes."

She was surprised. Leah and I stayed at Sarah's through Sunday afternoon. During those four days I got to see what her brother, Yaakov, was like. He was quiet but pleasant, helpful, respectful, positive, upbeat, and friendly. He played the piano and the guitar and had a wonderful voice. I myself love to sing. He was *frum*--religious--had nice parents, and came from a fine Jewish home with values similar to those with which I was raised. I got to see him in his natural setting; there wasn't any pretense. He seemed like a mensch, a person of integrity and honor.

On Sunday, one of my other roommates was hosting a surprise bridal shower, and Yaakov asked if he could drive me over. When he dropped me off, he asked me out for Monday. At that point, I had a set date to go out with Sam on Tuesday, but I had already decided over the holiday that I wasn't going to continue with Sam even if I had not met Yaakov.

Later that night when I arrived back home, I told Aunty how *Yom Tov* was and about Yaakov. I had only known him a few days, but he was sweet and seemed like someone you could trust. I said,

"I don't know if anything will come of it with this guy, but I could see myself marrying someone exactly like him."

Yaakov picked me up from the school library at noon on Monday. We went out for lunch at Jerusalem Pizza on Broadway, spent the rest of the day walking around the city, and then had dinner together as well. He brought me back to the dorm at 10 p.m.

I said, "Maybe you should call your mother and let her know where you are." He was a big boy and really didn't need to, but I felt that she might be wondering where he was. He went to make the call.

When he came back, he said that his mother had asked, "Don't you think it's time to come home?" To which he replied, "No." We giggled.

Ten hours for a first date--wow!

We started talking on the phone regularly and during our second date the following week, he bought me a freshwater pearl bracelet. It was very pretty. I thanked him but wouldn't accept it. I told him it was too soon. He seemed disappointed, but I think he understood. Yaakov had finished college the previous spring and was looking for a job working with computers. He sent out hundreds of resumés, but the field was flooded. I'm sure it must have been frustrating for him, but he always kept an upbeat and positive attitude. Six weeks after we met, Yaakov told me he loved me. This scared me but also made me happy. I wasn't ready to say the same back to him because I needed to feel certain, even though I believed that I already knew. The third day of *Chanukah*--surprise,

surprise--he gave me my bracelet. This time I accepted it. I had bought him a wallet. Two weeks later I told him that I loved him, too.

We knew that we were eventually going to get married. Yaakov would never have asked me to marry him if he hadn't had a means of supporting us. I still had another year of college to finish. The good news came in April 1985. Yaakov found a job as a computer consultant in New Jersey. He would have to make the hour-and-a-half trek there and back to Far Rockaway, New York, but at least he had finally found a job!

LIFE CHANGES

Perth Amboy was changing. For many years, the community had consisted of many Jewish families and a few *kosher* butcher shops. Years before, our *shul* had burned down. It had been built in 1905 and stood regally for close to eighty years. The adjacent store had an electrical fire and the *shul* caught fire, too. Several men ran inside, risking their lives to save the sacred *Torah* scrolls in the ark. Thank G-d, no one was hurt, and they got all the *Torahs* out safely. It truly was a sight to behold. The men's section had been on the ground floor and the women's in the balcony. On the holidays especially, the *shul* had been crowded with adults as well as children. The *shul* was and still is the central place where Jews congregate and socialize. In Perth Amboy, new businesses opened and old establishments closed. Different nationalities were moving into the area, and Spanish was becoming the popular language and culture we heard and saw on the street.

One evening when Daddy was walking home from the train station, as he did every day, he felt that he was being followed. He had had this strange sense over several days. He shared this with Uncle. By then, Aunty had retired and sold her store. She had owned her own business for twenty-eight years. Uncle advised him that perhaps it was time to move, but Daddy didn't want to move. He had a garden, albeit a small one, and grew tomato plants and green beans in his backyard. He didn't want to sell his house, but he felt the signs of change, too, and his house was sold.

Daddy wasn't going to buy another house at his age; he didn't need the responsibility of one anymore. He moved into a two-family house, renting the upstairs apartment from a friend of his. It was lovely, clean, and spacious, but Daddy could get restless if he wasn't occupied. He purchased a two-family house as an investment and rented it to two families. He eventually sold it and bought another house, again renting out the top- and bottom-floor apartments. Daddy was always a businessman with a sharp and creative mind.

In 1985, Arieh, Daddy's last remaining sibling, died. Daddy, Nomi, Laury, Magda, Hershey and I were the first people to arrive at the cemetery for Uncle Arieh's burial. Nomi asked Laury, "You saw *abba*?" and Laury responded, "I almost didn't recognize him without his glasses on."

Nomi was relieved when he saw her father because his body had been flown from Salt Lake City, Utah, and she wanted to make sure that it was the correct body. It was at that point that I saw my father become a bit wobbly and unbalanced. It was a warm day, but I was afraid for him. It was as if it had suddenly hit him that he was the last living member of his family. Uncle Arieh had been his last connection, his last bond to his immediate family. Thank G-d he still had his niece Nomi and his nephew Hershey.

Aunty and Uncle's fiftieth wedding anniversary was coming up, and I decided to give them a surprise party. I asked my cousins Hugo and Sissy if we could have it in their house, and they were delighted by this idea. Cousins and close friends were invited, as well as Yaakov, of course. My family liked Yaakov very much, and they saw where we were headed. The day of the party came and Aunty and Uncle were truly surprised. Aunty said she had suspected something, but not on this scale. She and Uncle were very happy.

September 22, 1985, was a picnic day. I put together a picnic basket, and Yaakov and I went to Roosevelt Park in Edison, New Jersey. It was a beautiful, warm day. We spread out on the ground a large blanket that Aunty had made years before by sewing together leftover strips of material from the dresses she had sold. We finished eating lunch, Yaakov took out dessert. It was a small, pretty round box with a ribbon. I gasped because I knew what it was--a beautiful engagement ring!

I started crying happy tears. We had been dating for eleven months, and I knew this was coming, but I couldn't believe it was finally here. We were very happy. We cleaned up, and since we were right across the street from the hospital, we wanted to go surprise Mommy. Yaakov had met Mommy a few times, and she liked him. I remember the first time that I told Yaakov about my mother. We had been dating for a month. He was very sweet and he shared something with me about his grandmother. I asked him if he had chosen this park because it was near Mommy, and he said that that had been part of the reason.

When we went into Mommy's room, the scene was perfect because Aunty, Uncle, and Daddy were there visiting. I put my left hand on the bar of Mommy's chair and we made small talk. Finally, Aunty noticed my hand with the shiny ring on it. With a huge smile on her face, she exclaimed, "They're engaged!" She started laughing, and Mommy started crying and laughing, and everyone was giving kisses and hugs all around.

We stayed a while longer, and Yaakov called his parents and made arrangements for us all to go to Yaakov's parents so that our families could meet. Sadly, Mommy couldn't come, but my future in-laws, Aaron and Cecily Dobin, would come down to meet my mother the following week.

When we arrived, my future father-in-law, Aaron, ran out to greet us. He hugged me fiercely, which at first surprised me. In religious circles, men and women do not have any physical contact before they are married. Once you are married, contact is solely between husband and wife. It doesn't include male relatives in your husband's family. It wasn't a foreign concept because in my family we always greeted our cousins with a peck on the cheek. It's something I would get used to out of respect for my father-in-law. My father laughed; he thought Aaron was Yaakov's brother because he looked so young. The truth is, my in-laws are, thank G-d, young and active, and young at heart. Yaakov and I were in the kitchen with his mother, and before dinner I wanted to tell my future mother-in-law that I was very happy to be marrying into this family. She hugged me and Yaakov.

My father told me later, "I am very proud that you are marrying into a religious family."

My father sat next to Aaron at the dining room table and he said to Daddy, "Your daughter has very good manners."

Daddy gushed, "That's because of her aunt."

He was right. Every manner or form of etiquette that I had learned came from Aunty. She had taught me and cared for me as if I were her own child. I remember that once, when I was about sixteen or seventeen years old, Aunty and I were in the kitchen talking while she was cooking. I accidentally called her Mommy. She looked right at me and said, "I am not your mother."

I said, "I know, Aunty; it was an accident. But you really are like my mother."

I hugged her. This role, which she was literally thrust into, took adjusting on her part, I'm sure. She was always good to me but strict because she felt she had to be. She had to adapt to a different kind of role now. She had a difficult time giving compliments and a difficult time accepting them, too. Two lovely compliments that she did give me were: "You were a beautiful bride," and "You are an excellent mother." Those words meant the world to me.

Wedding preparations abounded. There was much to do: buying a wedding gown and shoes, ordering flowers, hiring a photographer and a hall, etc. The most important question was: how will Mommy come to my wedding?

Aunty said, "How can Mommy be at the wedding?"

I said, "There's no way I'm getting married without Mommy there."

That was that. Daddy took care of all the arrangements. He hired an ambulette and an aide. Aunty and I went shopping for my gown, her gown, and a gown for Mommy. Aunty did the alterations for her gown and Mommy's gown. Mommy's cousin's daughter made headpieces for my mother and my aunt that matched their dresses.

Our special day came. The photographer and the caterer were very sensitive to our needs. By the time I was ready to walk down the aisle, Mommy had already been wheeled right up and in place under the *chuppah*, the wedding canopy. The back of the wheelchair had been draped in a black cloth to conceal it in the pictures. I was so glad to be able to hand my mother the *ketuba*, the Jewish marriage contract, after Yaakov had handed it to me. Later, during the dancing, I sat next to Mommy while a large group of men formed a circle and danced around us. It was a beautiful wedding and Mommy was so happy. At one point, Aaron put Daddy up on his shoulders and started dancing. That was a sight to see! Everyone was so happy, as it should be.

When Daddy saw me the next day I was wearing a beret on my head which covered all of my hair except for leaving out my bangs. Daddy exclaimed through laughter and tears, "You look like my Mamma."

After six months of marriage, I became pregnant with our first child. Yaakov and I were excited. We didn't tell anyone for the first three months because it is customary to wait until after the first trimester so as not to invite the evil eye. This might sound superstitious, but this is what most people do. The only ones we told within the first few weeks were our parents because they are our parents. Naturally, Mommy and Aunty cried. Daddy and Uncle smiled huge smiles. We drove out to Far Rockaway to tell my in-laws, and there were hugs all around.

A few months before my due date, Aunty and I were talking. She said *eem yirzeh Hashem*, G-d willing, if it was a boy she would like us to name him Dovid after her father. I didn't feel this would be a concern, and it's usual for the wife to choose the first-born's name, but I told her I would discuss it with Yaakov.

One memorable day in June 1987, was "labor day." Yaakov called his parents and Aunty to let them know we were at the hospital. Aunty asked Yaakov to call her every two hours. He said he didn't know if he could do that. Luckily, labor took only an hour and a half. Thank G-d, it was a quick and easy delivery and yes, it was a boy! He was six pounds, eight ounces. He had a full, full head of dark hair with even some strands hanging down. At birth, he was ready for his first haircut.

On the eighth day of a Jewish baby boy's life, barring any health complications, he has a *bris*, a circumcision. This command comes directly from the *Torah* when G-d made a covenant with Abraham that all his male descendants would enter into a sacred agreement with G-d for eternity. My father was the *sandek*, the one who holds the baby on his lap while the *mohel*, performs the circumcision. This was a great honor for my father. After the *bris* the name was called out: "*Dovid Yeshayahu ben Yaakov Tzvi*"(David Isaiah son of Jacob Tzvi.) Dovid is pronounced "Duv-id." Aunty was so happy and Daddy, too, because Yeshayahu was his father's name. How beautiful, and what a tribute to the memory of both grandfathers on my mother's and father's side to have a grandchild named after them. Later that day we went to tell Mommy in the hospital, and she was happy, too.

I had been teaching for just one year when I gave birth to Dovid. I knew that I wanted to be a stay-at-home mom, and thank G-d, my husband had a good job that allowed for that. I would often go to visit Mommy, and it gave her tremendous *nachas*, or pleasure, to watch Dovid grow. She was even able to hold him in her left arm. I remember that one Sunday we took her outside, and while she held him, he was sleeping. She said, "Come on, open your eyes," and she would nudge him a little and smile.

Mommy holding her first grandson, Dovid

THE ANNEX

One Sunday in June 1988, we went to see my mother in the new section of the hospital called The Annex, a section for the more serious cases. While Mommy was in the regular wing of Roosevelt, she had developed some kind of infection that caused open sores to form all over her body. The nurses gave us gloves and gowns, and we were told not to touch her while visiting because they were concerned it might be contagious. I thought it was ridiculous because this was my mother, but I listened because I had a child and had to think of him. I had never seen such a thing in my life. Gauze bandages covered parts of her arm, her cheek, and I don't remember where else. I asked the nurse if I could look underneath. There were raw, open sores. Her immune system had deteriorated and healing, if any, was very slow. Mommy was often sleepy, so I assumed she was on pain medication.

When Yaakov, Dovid, and I went to visit her one Sunday, the nurse said that we were not allowed to bring the baby in because Mommy could be contagious. Yaakov stayed in the lobby with Dovid, who had turned a year old three days earlier. We had brought him so that Mommy could see how big he was getting. She hadn't seen him in a while because of the infection. When I walked into her room, Mommy was wide awake and alert. She was in bed, as she had been for several weeks. She was quiet these days and hadn't spoken in a while. She followed me with her eyes as I came around to the left side of her bed. I didn't have gloves on, but I blew her kisses. She looked me up and down. I laughed. I said, "You notice I'm all dressed up. We just came from a *bar mitzvah*." I proceeded to tell her about it. She seemed to be listening and comprehending everything I was saying. I told her that Dovid's first birthday had been a few days ago and he was one year old now. Unbelievable! Mommy started crying. She was totally lucid. I saw that she was getting tired, so I blew her a kiss goodbye and told her that I loved her. Those were always the last words I would say when leaving her.

On June 24, Yaakov went to work as usual. I had just finished feeding Dovid breakfast when the phone rang. It was Daddy. "I'm very sorry to tell you, but Mommy died."

"Mommy died," I repeated. "What happened?"

Daddy said he didn't have time to talk because he had to start making arrangements. I hung up in shock. I knew how sick Mommy had been, but you think life will just continue the same way. You try not to think about the inevitable.

I suddenly began to scream, "Mommy's dead!" over and over. Dovid was looking at me like I was out of my mind, which I temporarily was. I held out my arms for him, but he seemed afraid and didn't come. My first reaction was to take my wedding album out from the bookshelf. I turned to the page of Mommy, Daddy and me. Mommy looked so beautiful and happy that day. I stared at her for a while, then put it away. I then called Yaakov and cried and he said how sorry he was. He came right home. I made some phone calls, but Daddy (and probably Aunty and Uncle) took care of the rest.

During the eulogy, Yaakov spoke. He said that I had asked him that morning after he had come home, "Do you think Mommy was proud of me?" He said that he was sure that she was. I was raising a Jewish family similar to the way she was raised. That night I had a dream about my mother. I was sitting on her hospital bed and she was sitting in her wheelchair. She was dressed all in white. Her hair was down and she looked very beautiful. We were talking but I didn't hear anything. The only words I heard her say about herself were, "I will not die." Then I woke up.

Strangely, I felt very comforted because I understood what she meant. She was telling me that as long as I talk about her and think about her, she will always be alive. I will always thank G-d for that dream because I believe with all my heart that He sent her to me via this dream to give me comfort during this very difficult period in my life. There's not a day that goes by that I don't see her face before me.

I know Mommy was forever grateful that her sister stepped in to raise me after she fell ill. After the burial I said to Aunty, "I feel like I'm losing my mind."

She said to me matter-of-factly, with no emotion, "You can't lose your mind; you have a child to take care of."

That did it. Those words snapped me back to reality. Aunty was now the only one left from her side of the Hecht family. She was the oldest and I believe, the strongest. She told me that when they were in the concentration camps, her younger sister, Roze (or Rozsika as they nicknamed her), looked at the morsel of food she had been given and scoffed, "What is this? I can't eat this." The little soup they were given to eat looked like it had sand in it. Aunty told her, "You have to eat whatever they give you." She had to be the strong one.

Thirteen months later, I became pregnant with my second child. My friends would ask me if I wanted a boy or a girl and I would reply, "It doesn't matter as long as the baby is healthy." But deep in my heart, I hoped that it would be a girl to name after my mother. This time, no one had any name requests because everyone, I believe, quietly knew what we would name the baby if it were a girl. This delivery was quite different from the first. Whereas Dovid came four days late, this baby was nine days late. My due date was over the Passover holiday, but I always joked that the *matzah*, unleavened bread, kept her stuffed in. When I went for my check-up, the doctor had trouble finding the heartbeat. She gave me a super-sugary drink of soda, and within minutes the baby was kicking up a storm, thank G-d! While I was in labor later that night, I was in a great deal of pain. I had brought a special prayer book with me that contained certain prayers to recite during labor. When Yaakov was sitting in the recliner and I was doing my breathing exercises, I would think of my mother while reciting these prayers, and the pain would subside—really! After four-and-a-half hours in labor (which I know is a blessing compared to some other stories I've heard), I was ready to deliver. When the doctor said, "It's a girl!" we were happy. Now we had one of each. My mother-in-law said I could put her in dresses and put ribbons in her hair. While I held the baby in the hospital I spoke to my mother and said, "Mommy, this is your namesake."

It was bittersweet. The baby looked like my mother. She had my mother's high cheekbones. Later, we saw that her personality matched my mother's as well--strong. She was born on a Wednesday, and on *Shabbos* we named her in *shul*. Her name is Rivka, my mother's Hebrew name. We call her Rivki.

A few months before my wedding, Uncle had had surgery to remove cancer from his prostate. He was seventy-seven years old. He recovered, but as time went on, he had other health issues. We were living in Highland Park, New Jersey, and were constantly begging my aunt and uncle to move to our town. We told them that they would love it in Highland Park, a wonderful Jewish community. They would have us for anything they needed, and would see the kids more often. Cousins Sissy and Hugo lived in Highland Park, there are several *shuls*, a butcher, bakery, etc. Sadly, there wasn't much Jewish life any longer in Perth Amboy. The elderly were either moving out, or unfortunately, dying. But Uncle didn't want to leave his garden.

It was a beautiful garden. Uncle had designed it and cared for it by himself for more than thirty-five years. He planted carrots, tomatoes, different types of beans, and gooseberries. He would proudly take me around through the maze of rows with all of the vegetables. He also had a lilac tree and rosebushes. Uncle had planted marigolds in deep stone boxes with a rough-textured exterior. He kept them on either side of the entrance to the front porch. Finally, there was a long row of daisies running the length of the driveway. He and Aunty would often cut flowers and put them in a vase on the kitchen and dining room tables. When Aunty would make green bean soup with milk, it was warm and comforting. The feelings I remember from these home-cooked meals were ones of warmth and love because all Aunty and Uncle did for me came from their hearts.

In 1991, almost two-and-a-half years after Rivki was born, I gave birth to another son. He came four days early and was my easiest birth of the three. Now it was Yaakov who had a name to give. Asher Anshel was Aaron's father's name. The day of the *bris* came, and Aaron was the *sandek* who had the honor of holding the baby on his lap while the *mohel* performed the circumcision. When the name was announced, I looked at my father-in-law and literally saw him breathe a sigh of relief. Now all the children in the Dobin and Gottesman families were named after a close, departed relative. What an honor to their memory.

Raising children with proper values, morals and ethics is a daily challenge. Yaakov and I were raised similarly in the ways of proper attributes, but differently in our way of approaching situations and challenges in life.

My family's experiences in the Holocaust made them fearful of new situations, especially my mother and aunt Ella. However unintentional, fear was instilled in me and I wasn't such an adventurous child. When I was learning to ride a bicycle, they only allowed me to ride in my backyard and in the parking lot next to my house when it was empty. I was never allowed to ride in the street. I grew up afraid to take chances. When roller skating or ice skating with a friend, I really tried, but fell often and lost confidence. When

I explained to Aunty my fear of trying something new, her response was, "I never told you not to do that."

"That may be true," I said, "but you made me afraid to try new things." She had no reply.

Only later in high school, and especially when I began attending college and chose to live in the dorm, did I really learn to fly. I made friends easily and discovered that I had a sense of humor. As much as I loved my family, it was a healthy distraction to live away from home, where I could finally achieve some independence and make my own decisions. I would go home almost every *Shabbos* where I would share my stories of all I did at school during the week, but I was happy to return to school.

When I met my husband, I saw in him an individual who was independent and confident in his abilities. As our relationship matured, he filled a void inside me. I began to feel more confident. He encouraged me to try new things and feel less fearful. Yaakov was raised with a healthy self-esteem and little fear of the unknown. In fact, he was quite the adventurous type. I told him after Dovid was born that this is how we should raise our children. We took the kids skating, swimming and biking and Yaakov took them skiing. I never let them know of my fears, but as teenagers they figured it out. Thankfully by then, they felt confident in their abilities to try new activities. Now when we go skating, Yaakov holds me up and the kids laugh playfully. They are glad to see me trying and they cheer me on. As I got older, I took on more leadership roles that helped me overcome my fears. Looking back on how I was raised by two individual women who possess strong personalities, I guess I am similar to both of these women in my life;

I enjoy socializing, dancing and reading. I became a teacher and [Yaakov and I are] quite active in our *shul*. Yaakov was the president of the *shul* for a couple of years and continues to be an active board member. I was on the sisterhood board for over nine years fundraising and programming events, then heading up the children's holiday *Simchat Torah* (Rejoicing with the Torah) program for ten years, and then I led the kindergarten *Shabbos* program for six years. Both my mother and my Aunt Ella had a profound effect and influence on my life.

As the years went on, I saw in my children a certain shyness when it came to making friends. I encouraged playdates and had company often for *Shabbos* meals. As young adults, my children have become more social. Dovid is our *shul* Director of Teen Programming, and works as a manager of a thriving business. He is well-liked and respected. Rivki attended graduate school, got married, and is the proud mother of a beautiful baby girl. She is the music teacher in a *yeshiva* and gives private piano and guitar lessons to adolescents. She, too, married a man who is similar to her father- friendly, social and active in the community. Our younger son Asher is very well-liked. He has become quite popular in college. He sits on the student government and is active in school related extra curricular activities such as visiting and singing with a group of his college friends for the patients in a nursing home. He is kind to everyone and can be relied upon to lend a helping hand. We are very proud of all of our children's accomplishments.

UNCLE

In 1994, Uncle's health started to deteriorate. His hands started to shake. He was diagnosed with Parkinson's disease. One day, we received a call from the police that there had been a minor accident. Uncle's car had veered over a fork in the road. Thank G-d, no one was hurt. The officer asked Uncle how old he was.

"Eighty-four."

The officer said it was time for Uncle to give up driving. This was devastating for Uncle, but he listened. His car sat in the garage until he sold it. He soon was in need of a cane and eventually, a walker. He could no longer walk to *shul* and would *daven* at home. Uncle began to lose weight. He couldn't hold down solids easily, and getting proper nutrition became a problem. He no longer could care for his garden in his backyard and it became overgrown with weeds.

Because I was a stay-at-home mom for six years, I was able to visit Aunty and Uncle twice a week to help them with grocery shopping and take them to their doctor appointments. When Dovid was a baby, I would bring along his bathtub so Aunty could help me bathe him. Even though I didn't need her help, it made her happy to share in different aspects of our daily routine.

In May 1995, Uncle had to be admitted to the hospital. He could no longer keep food down. The doctors planned to put in a feeding tube. Uncle was in the hospital for a few days before the surgery, and I went to visit him early one morning. He had a big smile for me; he always did. No matter how uncomfortable he was or how ill he felt, he rarely complained. He never liked being the focus of conversation or attention. While visiting I talked about what each of the kids was up to in school and all of the funny things Asher said. Asher was three-and-a-half, Rivki had just turned six, and Dovid was almost eight years old. When I said goodbye, he said, "So soon?"

I explained that Asher would be home from school shortly and that I would be back again to visit. I kissed him and told him that I loved him.

The next day, the feeding tube was put in and Uncle lapsed into a coma. Aunty stayed with him most of the day, and then I brought her back to my house to sleep. We had a long talk. I told her that of course we should *daven* that Uncle should recuperate and come home soon, but if he would not get well, that *Hashem* should take him so that he wouldn't suffer anymore. Aunty stayed by his bedside all day on Wednesday and slept at the hospital. Our phone rang around four thirty a.m. and the nurse told me that

Uncle had passed away. She asked me to come pick up Aunty who was sitting next to Uncle's bed. She said, "This woman just lost the love of her life."

She had no idea how true that statement was.

Uncle was taken to the funeral home. Jewish custom dictates that a deceased person's body should not be left unattended between death and burial. People usually take shifts sitting with the body and reciting *Tehillim*, Psalms. I sat beside him and recited *Tehillim* and spoke to him. Before a Jewish person is buried, he or she is immersed in a *mikvah*, a ritual bath of rainwater for purification purposes, then dressed in handmade white shrouds that cover the body from head to toe. Before the funeral began, Aunty wanted to see Uncle one last time. Aunty looked at him and said, "He looks like he's sleeping. Isadore, why did you leave me?"

We slowly closed the pine casket and took our seats. It was time for the *hesped* (eulogy). Only Uncle's rabbi spoke, and then I spoke. I needed to express the numerous thoughts and feelings that I had for this man who was not my blood relative, but to whom I could not have felt closer had he been my own father.

Aunty and Uncle with baby Miriam

My Uncle Isadore was a very special man; he was a very exceptional, unique man. He was kind and dear, generous, loving, caring. A very soft-spoken man. He had a lot of patience and always a kind word for everyone. With no disrespect to my own father, my Uncle Isadore was really like a father to me. When I was ten years old, my mother, may she rest in peace, had a stroke and had to be hospitalized, and she stayed in the hospital, on and off, for the next fourteen years. My father worked and came home late at night, so who would take care of a ten-year-old? Without a question or a thought, my Aunt Ella and Uncle Isadore took me into their home and raised me. In essence, I had four parents. Aunty and Uncle, unfortunately, didn't have their own children, but they were very natural at being parents with their kind and nurturing manner.

Uncle and I had a very special relationship. I remember how Uncle would always sit with me and help me with my homework after a long day of work. He would take me to school every day. But what stands out most in my mind was what a truly religious man he was.

My uncle survived the Holocaust--he alone of his parents and seven brothers and sisters. Thank G-d, he had Aunty. They were married for nine years before the war, and it was a true miracle that they both survived to come back to each other. He came from a strictly Orthodox home and had a vast amount of knowledge of the *Torah* and secular studies. In Europe, he would have a study partner to learn some portion of the *Torah* with him every week. He was a smart man with a very sharp and focused mind. With every lesson he taught me or wanted to explain to me, always, always he would quote some words from the *Torah*, our sacred Jewish book of law. He would never miss a day of going to *shul* to *daven* with a *minyan* three times a day. Many times when we would be relaxing at home, I would see him getting up to go to take a *Chumash* or a *Mishna* to look something up for whatever he was just thinking about.

When he was weak and not feeling up to going to *shul*, he went about his daily business. But you could see he always looked forward to his daily prayers. He was a real *ba'al chesed*, a very kind and generous man. He would give to many of the charities that came to his attention. He kept a strictly *kosher* home in and out, and was *Shomer Shabbat*, a Sabbath observer. He fully lived the life of a true Orthodox Jew. He was a real *Yiddishe mensch*, a true Jewish being of integrity and honor.

The most important and meaningful aspect of his life his whole life, was my Aunt Ella. She was everything to him-- his wife, his best friend. They were married for sixty years. They lived a full, rich life with one another. They lived modestly because that's the type of couple they were. As I mentioned earlier, they had no children of their own, yet *Hashem* works in ways we have no understanding of. They raised me and now, thank G-d, I have a wonderful family of my own: my husband, Yaakov, and our children, Dovid, Rivki, and Asher. My uncle and Yaakov had a very nice relationship, and how deeply he loved our children.

The last time I spoke with my uncle was on May 4th, two days before he went into a coma. He was weak and it was a bit hard for him to speak. Even though he was uncomfortable, he nevertheless asked and spoke about Yaakov and the children. I told him that Rivki had just turned six years old, and that Dovid was doing well in school, and the funny things Asher was doing. And he was so happy and smiling, and I just kept telling him to think positive thoughts and to get well for all of us. This past Tuesday, my aunt and I were saying that Uncle was really in *Hashem*'s hands now, and if he were going to get well, then we hoped that *Hashem* would cure him. If not, we hoped that He would just take Uncle so that there would be no more suffering for everyone involved. Early Wednesday morning, Aunty called to say that he was gone. *Hashem* had answered us. When we think about Uncle, we will always remember how funny, sweet, thoughtful, and kind he was to everyone. Anyone who knew him, loved him. We love you, Uncle, and you will be in our hearts and minds forever.

When my mother died, Daddy had a double headstone erected. Aunty and Uncle had purchased plots in a different section of the cemetery, but they decided that they wanted all four of them to be buried alongside each other, so Aunty and Uncle purchased plots next to my parents. Today, they are all together.

Uncle was a very practical and intelligent man. He had several sayings or expressions he would share. I learned much from these simple words about how to conduct myself with others. When shopping or talking with someone, he would say, "Give me the best and the cheapest." If I were running late for something, he would say, "Better that I should wait for someone rather than that he should wait for me." When I began driving, he would say, "I trust you. I don't trust the driver in front of you or the driver in back of you." When visiting us once, I gave him a cup of water that was not quite full, and he said, "Miriamkela, don't feel sorry for the water." And whenever I would complain about the taste of some foods, he would say, "Miriamkela, you eat to live, not live to eat."

When my son, Dovid, was about seven years old, he noticed Uncle's left arm and pointing, he asked, "What's that?"

Uncle instinctively covered with his right hand the number on his arm--the number that fifty years earlier had been burned into his arm by the Nazi soldiers in the Auschwitz concentration camp during World War II, during the Holocaust.

He looked away.

I said, "Uncle, it's okay. You're going to have to explain it to him one day." He remained silent, and had a sad and distant look on his face as he stared straight ahead. He had done nothing wrong; there was nothing to be ashamed of. He had just had the privilege of being born Jewish. My mother, father, aunt, and uncle always, from beginning to the end of their lives, were proud Jews.

There is a moving and poignant children's book called, *The Number On My Grandfather's Arm*, by David A. Adler. As an educator, a mother, and a child of Holocaust survivors, I highly recommend it for children from second grade and up. After this quiet moment with Uncle, I went to the library, took out this book, and sat down with Dovid to read it to him. I explained that Uncle, Aunty, Bubby and Zaidy were imprisoned although they had done nothing wrong. I said that there are some people in this world who don't like Jews, and it isn't right. I told him that our family is proud to be Jewish as he should always be proud of being Jewish.

Uncle Isadore had been in two concentration camps: first, Auschwitz in Poland, and later, Dachau in Germany. When Aunty and Uncle arrived at the Auschwitz concentration camp, they came packed into cattle cars. One hundred people could be squeezed into each car. They were shouted out of the cattle car. Men and women were separated. Children went with their mothers. Little did they know, but Aunty and Uncle were not to see each other again for over a year.

Uncle was given a job working by the crematorium. A friend got him a different, much better job working in the stables with the officers' horses. The friend explained that if he stayed by the ovens, that's where he would wind up. Uncle's left arm had been tattooed with numbers in blue ink. I have seen letters with the digits on other survivors' arms. Thinking back now, I believe there was an A alongside the numbers, possibly to signify that he was in Auschwitz. While writing, I began looking through old photo albums with pictures from my parents and aunt and uncle's youth. I came across a picture of Uncle when he was visiting Yaakov and me in our apartment back in the late 1980s and remarkably, there was a picture of him alone, wearing a short-sleeve shirt, his left arm exposed, and his tattoo clearly showing. We scanned the picture into the computer and this was the number that was cruelly tattooed onto his arm:

A-13552

I searched online for records about my Uncle's on the **Auschwitz Prisoner Search** list of prisoners, and there it was: Reich, Isidore, June 1, 1909, A-13552.

Innocent people were reduced to numbers, no longer allowed to have a name, an identity. That is why the Holocaust Memorial in Israel is called *Yad Vashem*, literally, a hand and a name, an idiom that refers to the individualness and uniqueness of every person. This returns to each and every one his or her name to be memorialized, together with stories of all those who survived, as well as those who perished.

Women and children had also been tattooed, but my mother and aunt didn't have numbers. I don't know why some people received tattoos and others didn't.

Yaakov and I took a trip to Washington, DC, in December 2012 and visited the Holocaust Museum. We had been there several years earlier, but now I was interested in getting answers to some of my questions. A very knowledgeable gentleman explained to us that the people who didn't receive tattoos on their forearm were "in transit," meaning that they were in Auschwitz temporarily until they were moved to another camp location for "work." This was true. After four months in Auschwitz and a "selection," my mother and aunt, who had been selected for the right line (which meant life) were transported to Nuremberg. (As you may recall, my brave mother had been chosen to go left, which meant death, but ran to the right line and miraculously survived).

Uncle had further described what went on. He said the guards would wake up the men in the barracks at midnight, make them line up, and force them to just count out loud aimlessly. In the morning when he went to the washroom, he would see a pile of dead bodies stacked from floor to ceiling. He said that he didn't care if he lived or died.

When the war was over, and the Americans had liberated Dachau in the spring of 1945 (Auschwitz had been liberated by the Russians in winter 1945), the American soldiers asked Uncle where he wanted to go. He said that he wanted to rest. He was weak so he went to a Displaced Person (DP) camp for a month. He had no idea if his wife, Ella, was alive or not, but he knew that his parents--four brothers and two sisters --were gone, murdered by the Nazis in 1942.

Uncle made his way back to Galszecs (Galsij) in Czechoslovakia where he and Aunty had been living before being forced to go into hiding in 1942. As Jews were returning, the townspeople were calling out to them, "There are more of you coming back than were taken away!"

Aunty and Uncle had been tenants of the Wintners, a Jewish family that employed Uncle in their textile factory. When Uncle returned they were very happy, although shocked, that he was alive. Mrs. Wintner took his clothes and burned them because they were infested with lice. Uncle was so weak that she had to spoon feed and nurse him back to health. As Jews returned to Galszecs, Uncle would inquire about Ella Reich. Soon, Uncle received word that Aunty was alive and coming home!

When Uncle's strength returned, he traveled to his parents' home to pack up and see what furniture and belongings he would take back, and what he could sell. What a shock it was for him to find, not an empty house, but a house inhabited by their former neighbors! When the Jews were carted away, the neighbors had moved into the Reich family home and were using all their belongings as if they were theirs--*thieves*! Uncle said the people were scared. The wife begged him not to throw them out, and tried to hand him a chicken. The sad truth is that numerous individuals returning to their homes after the war experienced the same shock as my uncle did.

Uncle left the house, found a man whom he knew from town, and made a deal with him. He said, "I will sell you my house, but you must throw these people out." The man agreed, this is what they did.

When Uncle was healthier, he went back to work for Mr. Wintner in his store. Mr. Wintner gave him money to start his own business, saying: "Here is some money. Now start to live again!" What truly loving and generous people. After Aunty and Uncle had emigrated to the United States in 1949, and for many years afterwards, they still kept in touch with the Wintners and their sons.

My mother and Aunty and Uncle all stayed together. Mommy and Aunty had an uncle who lived in Pittsburgh, Pennsylvania, and he became their sponsor. They applied for sponsorship after the war, and it took more than three-and-a-half years before they were granted the right to emigrate.

I know Uncle was a strong Zionist in his heart. Had Israel not been a fledgling state acquiring its rebirth in 1948, I believe that he, Aunty, and possibly, my mother, would have emigrated there after the war. However, because everything was so unsure, they chose to come to the United States where they had family and a new beginning.

Aunty and Uncle visited Israel for the first time in 1967 after the Six Day War, when the Israelis recaptured Jerusalem from Arab domination and rightfully returned it to Jewish hands. They loved Israel. In 1973, after the Yom Kippur war, they visited again and were seriously thinking about moving there, but life doesn't always go in the direction you would like. My mother had had a stroke and there was no more talk of moving. Aunty wouldn't leave her sister.

Olga and Ella

A NEW BEGINNING, A FRESH START ON LIFE

Aunty aged considerably after Uncle died: Her hair quickly turned much grayer. She didn't like to be alone and felt insecure. What had happened to this strong woman who raised me and was the big sister for her five siblings?

Shortly after Aunty got up from *shiva*, a seven-day period of mourning, Yaakov and I told her we wanted her to move to Highland Park to be near us. She wasn't a youngster and should not be alone.

During the summer of 1995, she told us that her next-door neighbor had shot her husband in their basement. That was it. We put the house up for sale within the week. I picked her up several times to go apartment hunting. We looked at many places and came across a beautiful condominium complex. It was spacious for one person, and allowed for much sunlight. It was also one block from a *shul*. She said, amidst tears, "Oh, Isadore would have loved this." We moved her in at the end of December 1995. There were several widows in the building whom Aunty easily befriended. She had never had so many companions, and was very, very happy in her new home. Best of all, she lived within a mile of us.

In the same year, Mommy and Aunty's first cousin, Hugo Princz, brought a lawsuit against the German government. He also sued IG Farben Chemical Industry Conglomerate for having collaborated with the German government in the production of Zyklon B gas, whose sole purpose was to gas Jews in the Auschwitz concentration camp. This gas replaced the water that would normally have come from the showerheads. These lawsuits were filed during the Clinton administration. Hugo met with the President and told him that he needed to put pressure on the Germans.

Hugo's father was born in Czechoslovakia and came to the United States for work. While he was here, became a U.S. citizen. When he returned to Europe, all his future children automatically became U.S. citizens. Hugo, born after his father's return, was therefore legally an American. When the Nazis entered Czechoslovakia in 1942 and rounded up the Jews, Hugo presented proof that he was an American citizen, but the Nazis ignored it. All they saw was a man who was a Jew, and he was put in concentration camps.

At my wedding in March 1986, Hugo met someone who put him in touch with a lawyer whose law firm specialized in seeking compensation for Holocaust survivors for their horrific experiences, enslavement, loss of loved ones, and forced labor during the years of persecution. It took time, but Hugo eventually won both his battle, and the battle for all Holocaust survivors.

Aunty and I filled out paperwork and submitted it to the Jewish Claims Conference. She also received compensation for her time in the ghetto. She already required a full-time home health aide, and the quarterly stipend helped her, to some extent, in her older years.

That same year, 1995, in addition to losing Uncle, Aunty suffered another trauma. Aunty found out that she had breast cancer. Her doctor discovered a lump in her right breast and said that he would perform a lumpectomy. Aunty had been so involved with Uncle that she had ignored her own health. She was so upset with herself. We scheduled an appointment as quickly as possible, and the procedure was done. The doctor explained what he had done and prescribed an oral medication that she had to take daily for the next five years. That was it and what a blessing--no radiation or chemotherapy. He removed the cancerous tumor and she lived normally for the next eight years of her life.

While visiting Aunty one day in August 1996, I saw an article in a Jewish newspaper that was sitting on her dining room table about offices that had been set up for Holocaust survivors to call to request that a representative come to their home to videotape them while they answered questions and told stories of what life was like before, during, and after their experiences in the Holocaust. These offices were set up around the world to get as many survivors' stories as possible on videotape as an educational and historical tool. The program had been put together by film director Steven Spielberg after he had completed his film, Schindler's List. The goal was to pass the survivors' legacy down to future generations. A representative came to videotape Aunt Ella the following week. One year later, my father was videotaped as well. My family now has these precious tapes to pass on.

Shortly after we had moved Aunty to Highland Park to be close to us, I was visiting her and saw an interesting article in one of the local Jewish newspapers about suing the German and Swiss governments for Holocaust reparations. I called the phone number in the article and the Jewish Claims Conference sent us the application. Aunty said that her father hadn't had any Swiss bank accounts, but the attorneys working with these foreign governments said that we should write down anything of value that had been stolen. Aunty said sarcastically, "I should write: 'My father's gold fillings in his teeth.'"

A few months later, Aunty received an envelope from the Jewish Claims Conference. I opened it and pulled out a check from the Swiss banks for $1,000!

I said, "Aunty, you're not going to believe this."

I showed her the check and her initial reaction was, "You're kidding!"

She took it and began sobbing.

"This is worth nothing," she said. No amount of money could ever compensate for her father's stolen life.

July 12, 1998, was a day that turned our lives upside down. It wasn't a typical Sunday because it was the fast day of *Shiva Assar B'Tammuz*-- the seventeenth day in the Jewish month of Tammuz. This date on the Jewish calendar begins a three week period when nothing festive or joyous is celebrated. Weddings, concerts, parties-- even shaving one's beard and haircuts--cease during this time. This observance dates back to 586 BCE, when the first Temple in Jerusalem was destroyed. I received a call from a nurse in the emergency room of our nearby hospital that a Mr. Morris Gottesman had been brought in by helivac. It had taken them two hours to finally get my name from him because he had no identification on him. I told them that we would be there soon. My first thought was, "What could have happened to Daddy?" He would be ninety-one years old one month later.

When we arrived at the emergency room, Daddy appeared fine. In fact, he was so angry that he had had to be restrained. The nurse explained that it was a good thing we hadn't seen him when he first came in. She described all the blood that had been coming from his skull. It seemed that Daddy had fallen while tending to his tomato plants in back of the *shul*. No one was clear about how it had occurred--whether he tripped on the stairs, passed out, or had a mini- stroke--but on his way to get the garden hose from the basement of the *shul*, Daddy had fallen down fifteen concrete steps. By some miracle, he had walked up the stairs covered with blood and screamed for help. Luckily, a neighbor had heard him and called 911. Daddy was transported by helicopter to the trauma center of the hospital. These were his injuries: open skull fracture, bleeding on the right side of the brain, collapsed right lung, broken right arm, and broken bone under the right eye. He is a miracle man! This diminutive, 5-foot-tall man was unbelievably high in stature. He couldn't be put down, nor would he allow himself to be put down. It seems clear that G-d wanted him on this earth for a very long time.

My father had been restrained because he kept trying and trying to stand up, of course. When he saw Yaakov he said, "Yaakov, get a knife and cut the ropes."

Yaakov said, "I can't do that."

Poor Yaakov, he didn't know what to do. I, on the other hand, stepped out of the room and, G-d should forgive me, let out some nervous chuckles. This was my father's nature. He was a fighter through and through. I thanked G-d that through a miracle Daddy was alive, and I knew he would come out of this.

The following day I went to Perth Amboy to meet the neighbor that lived next to the *shul*. I introduced myself, and she explained what had happened when she had heard a man yelling for help. I thanked her for her kindness and went to the backyard of the *shul*. I took a few steps down the stairs where my father had fallen, and saw a swarm of mosquitoes swirling around a pool of dried blood. This event had happened so suddenly that I didn't know how to react. I felt harried because I now had so many new responsibilities to take on. When Mommy became ill, Daddy, Aunty and Uncle took care of all the details. When Uncle fell ill, Aunty took care of all the details. Now it was my turn. I had to pull myself together, but I also needed help. One of the services of the *bikur cholim*, a Jewish organization that helps the sick and those in need, is to prepare meals for the families of the infirm individual. For almost two weeks, people cooked and sent us meals to lighten the load, and it was truly appreciated.

My first cousin Nomi and her husband Laury, from Salt Lake City, Utah, happened to be visiting relatives on the East Coast at the time. They came to visit Daddy. Hershey, Daddy's nephew, and his wife, Magda, also came. They lived in Queens, New York. Hershey was Daddy's deceased older brother's son. In addition to having lost five siblings before the Holocaust, my father also lost his parents and two more siblings, Yisrael and Sarah, during the Holocaust. They were murdered in Auschwitz.

Yisrael had been a furrier, married to Rachel. In 1926, they had one child, a son, named Tzvi Hersh, whom we call Hershey. He had helped his father with the business. He was eighteen when he was sent to Auschwitz and remained incarcerated there for one year. He was young and strong. The way he survived is incredible in itself. Toward the end of the war, in 1945, Hershey became very skinny. Miraculously, during an *appel* when the prisoners had to line up for a selection, he was able to avoid being sent to the crematoria by lying down among the dead bodies. He was so emaciated he could pass for one of the dead. He survived his parents.

In 1945, after the war, Hershey moved to Israel and lived there for seven years. He then went to Canada, met his wife, Magda, and they emigrated to the United States in 1957. They owned a store in Manhattan selling discounted variety merchandise. They have three children: Elizabeth (Liz), Eveline, and Steven.

My father's one remaining sibling, Arieh, had been living in Palestine (as it was called at the time) and had passed away more than twenty-five years before. Arieh was twenty-three when he travelled from Svalyava to Prague to become more knowledgeable about business. He too, became a more secular Jew and in 1933, he emigrated to Palestine because he was a Zionist. In 1941 he met his future wife, Reny, and in December 1944 they had their one child, a daughter, called Nomi. Arieh had a small store in the center of Tel Aviv where he sold women's wear. On January 1, 1959, the family emigrated to the United States, settling in New York. Years later,

Reny died, shortly before Nomi's first child was born. Arieh then moved to Salt Lake City, Utah, to live near Nomi and her family.

Nomi and Hershey are my two first cousins. We are each close to twenty years apart, and each have three children of our own, thank G-d. We are a small family on the Gottesman side. I can only imagine what a large family I would have had, with many aunts, uncles, and cousins, had the inhuman tragedy of the Holocaust never been allowed to happen.

Three weeks after his fall, Daddy was transferred to a rehabilitation facility. The owner happened to be an Orthodox Jew and he ordered in *kosher* food for my father. He also helped my father wrap *tefillin,* phylacteries, around his arm in the morning. He was very kind to my father.

During this time, Yaakov and I spoke with Daddy and told him that it was time to move to Highland Park to be near us and the children. He agreed, thank goodness. We began cleaning out his apartment in Perth Amboy. What a huge job that was! Daddy had saved everything-- and I mean *everything*. I'm sure much of this mentality came from being a Holocaust survivor because after the war, he literally had nothing--no family, no belongings, no money-- nothing. He had to start life over again. In fact, when he left Europe to come to the United States, he brought goose pillows and blankets because he didn't know what he could get here.

While my father was in the rehabilitation facility, a CAT scan disclosed that there was water accumulating on his brain and he had to have surgery to drain it. Luckily, the procedure was successful, but he couldn't return to the facility afterwards because there were no available beds. We opted for a facility that was further from home because there he could receive physical therapy and occupational therapy--*huge mistake*!

I visited Daddy a few times a week and did not like what I saw. His arm was still in a cast, which made opening the meals, plus cutting and eating the food on his own almost impossible. The food tray laid unopened and untouched, so I offered to feed him. He was so frustrated and angry to be there that he didn't eat. I reported this to the director and she said it would be taken care of. However, at my next visit, it was the same situation: The tray just sat there, unopened. I began taking Daddy to a local *kosher* pizza shop, where he had a decent meal. He was losing weight and we didn't know what to do. On top of this, he wasn't going to the therapies he was entitled to and the therapist's attitude was, "If he doesn't want to go I'm not going to force him."

The following week was *Rosh Hashana*. I got in touch with the local synagogue, and they assured me that someone would come by to blow *shofar*, sounding the ram's horn to usher in the Jewish New Year, for Mr. Gottesman. I told Daddy that *Rosh Hashana* would be in a few days and that someone would come to blow *shofar* for him.

Erev Rosh Hashana I was busy preparing for my household and was about to light candles to welcome in the *Yom Tov* when the phone rang. "Mrs. Dobin? This is the nurse from the nursing home. Your father was found walking along the highway by state troopers and brought back to the facility."

"What! How could you have let this happen? How was he able to walk out when there is security?" I replied. The nurse responded, "Your father was dressed like a visitor and he broke the ankle bracelet off of his foot." This was insane.

After the holiday was over, I went to visit Daddy. I asked if someone had come to blow *shofar* for him and he said, "Yes."

Then I asked him why he had been walking along the highway. Matter-of-factly he answered, "I got dressed to go to *shul* for *Rosh Hashana* (slacks, shirt and jacket: that was all he had with him), and the officers saw me and gave me a ride. They were so nice to me."

Enough was enough. This was a terrible predicament. I asked if he would like to come home, and naturally, he said yes.

Thanks to our rabbi's connections, we found an apartment near our home, but it wouldn't be ready for six weeks, so Daddy lived with us during this time. My daughter Rivki, who was nine years old, gave up her room for her *zaidy*. She slept on the sofa bed in the living room. It wasn't easy, but she didn't complain. How oddly reminiscent this situation was of mine so many years ago. She understood that this was temporary and enjoyed having her *zaidy* in our home; so did Dovid and Asher. The main thing was that now he was safe and eating well. All three kids would come home from school with a big kiss for their *zaidy* and a hug. Yaakov and I had to go to work, so we hired a part-time male aide. He was wonderful and most of all, patient.

November came and Daddy moved into his own apartment, but he could no longer live alone. He needed round-the-clock care.

We hired a full-time aide, but she was sneaky and wanted a large amount of money to stay. Otherwise, she would leave. She used my father's illness to her advantage, so we hired someone else and let her go. The women we hired couldn't care for him because they were afraid of his mood swings. The doctor said these were signs of dementia. Daddy's demeanor began to change. He would hallucinate and became paranoid. Once, in the middle of the night, the aide called our home crying hysterically and saying that she was afraid. Yaakov took the phone and spoke to Daddy who said, "Yaakov, come quick. There are people in the basement, they are trapped, they can't get out. We have to help them!" Daddy was speaking hurriedly and frantically. Yes, this was a hallucination, but tragically, these visions were also the truth. While my father was in forced labor camps in Yugoslavia, this horrific event occurred. Eight Jewish boys who were trying to run away to the Partisans were caught stealing food and were put in a basement, or as Daddy would describe it, a dungeon. They were there for a long time and eventually were shot to death before my father's eyes, as well as in front of all the units in the forced labor camp. Thank G-d for my husband. He told Daddy to calm down and said he would be right over. I stayed home with the children who were asleep. It was two-o-clock in the morning. Yaakov returned over an hour later. He had showed Daddy that the closet was empty, and explained to him that everyone was safe, that no one was in danger. He helped him back to bed and came home. The aide was very grateful.

Sadly, the same thing happened the following night. After these two episodes, the doctor prescribed medicine to keep him calm and he did well on it. I visited Daddy daily after work and he seemed to be well cared for. He was clean, dressed well, and seemed to be eating properly. His memory was pretty decent, and we enjoyed having his company every other *Shabbos* while his aide had the day off. He spent all the holidays with us and she joined us as well, to help Daddy. She stayed with my father for four-and- a-half years, until he died.

Shabbos was very special for the kids. We were all together at *shul*, and then Yaakov would push Daddy in the wheelchair as we walked home. When we arrived home, we enjoyed our lunch around the dining room table in honor of *Shabbos*. Daddy would sing *zemiros* like he used to, and we would share with him all that had gone on during the week. When lunch was over, Daddy would make an A-OK sign and shake his wrist, with a sweet smile, telling me, "Thank you very much, it was very good." Afterwards, he took a nap on the couch, and later on the kids would play a game of catch with a soft ball and some card games with their *zaidy*.

My father had wrestled with religion on and off after the war's end, but certain traditions never left him. The type of woman he had chosen to marry reflected the way his home had been back in Europe. My mother had made a *kosher* and *shomer Shabbos* home for him. However, in the United States, Daddy felt that in order to put bread on the table, he needed to work on *Shabbos*. So while he was working on Saturday, Mommy and I were at home. I received so many mixed signals about being religious. I went to *yeshiva* where we learned that you don't do any work on the Shabbat, yet my father did work on *Shabbos*. I recall a conversation between Daddy and his nephew, Hershey. Hershey said to Daddy in amazement, "I don't understand how you could have such a religious daughter!"

After my father's fall down the stairs, he started becoming stronger in his religious observance. When we visited him, he would often have a *siddur* open and would *daven* from any page. He went to *shul* every *Shabbos*, but during the week his aide kept a *siddur* on the table for him. When I was still a young child, I had noticed this transition after he had stopped working on *Shabbos*. He was returning to his roots. I strongly believe that however you start out in life, no matter what other roads you may take, there is a force that pushes you back to the beginning. At least, this is what happened to my father.

One day in September 2003, I received early morning a call from the aide, who had called 911 because Daddy was having difficulty breathing. I told her that she had done the right thing. I went in the ambulance with Daddy, and he was put in the Intensive Care Unit [ICU]. I stayed with him for several hours until I had spoken with his doctors and he was stabilized. Daddy was in the ICU for a few days.

When my father was brought in, he was wearing of all things, a beautiful, thick gold ring that he had brought over from Europe. It had his initials, A and G, engraved and intertwined on the face of the ring: A for Abraham and G for Gottesman. The nurse saw it and was very sensitive to this. She used soapy water to remove it from his finger--"so it shouldn't get stolen"--and handed it to me. I thanked her kindly. It's a very special ring and we cherish it to this day.

When Yaakov and I went to visit Daddy before going to work, he said to Yaakov, "I'm going to die." Yaakov reassured him that that wasn't going to happen. By the third day, the nurse was even feeding him applesauce. Later that day, someone from the hospital called to say that Daddy would have to be placed on a ventilator and asked what we wanted to do. Daddy had a Living Will giving me permission to have authority over all medical decisions regarding his welfare. It was a great burden to have to make such decisions. According to Jewish law, you are not allowed to withhold air, water or food from a person. There was no choice but to put Daddy on a ventilator. The doctor could prescribe medication to keep him comfortable but could not give him morphine to speed up death. It was up to G-d when to take Daddy.

I was in constant contact with the doctor as well as with our rabbi. In fact, he and the doctor met at the hospital and discussed my father's situation. They had respect for one another's point of view. The doctor tried a few times to wean Daddy off the ventilator, but Daddy was too weak and couldn't breathe on his own for long periods. Our routine every day was for Yaakov to visit Daddy before he went to work, and for me to visit Daddy after I finished work. The kids were still in school, so that was one less thing to worry about. This was our pattern for the next six weeks.

HASHEM MUST LOVE ME—I'M BEING TESTED CONSTANTLY

One Sunday morning while speaking by phone with Aunty, her speech sounded slurred, as if she were groggy. I told her that I didn't want to scare her, but it sounded to me as if she were having a stroke. Fortunately, I had recognized the signs, and told her that I would be right over. When I saw her, the right side of her face was drooping, her right eyelid was partly closed, and her speech was slurred. I asked her to sit down. She said that she felt fine. Nevertheless, I went with my gut instinct and called a doctor. I described her symptoms and he said that it sounded like Bell's Palsy and we should go right to the emergency room. Bell's Palsy, we learned, is like a mini-stroke, and if it is caught within the first three hours of the initial symptoms, medication can be administered by injection to prevent any damage. We had no idea how long she had been in this state, so they could only keep her for observation. This was our situation: my father was on a ventilator on the respiratory care floor of the hospital, and now my aunt was in the emergency room of the same hospital.

After Aunty had been admitted, I went to see Daddy, and unbelievable as this may sound, when I stepped out of his room for a few minutes to stretch and walk around, directly across the hall I saw Aunty in bed in her own room! G-d truly had mercy on me so that I wouldn't have to run around, and could be attentive to both of them at the same time.

Aunty was released after only a few days and, thank G-d, her symptoms went away, but she didn't feel comfortable living alone anymore. She was scared. We signed up for a special service for her.

If you fall or aren't feeling well, you press a button on a specialized wristwatch that alerts a central system to a possible emergency. Even though she never needed to use it, she still felt this wasn't enough security for her. My father's aide was still living in his apartment in hope that Daddy would recuperate and come back home. She therefore could stay several hours a day with Aunty to help her cook and clean, go for walks, and be her companion.

The High Holidays were now here and they were very emotional. On *erev Yom Kippur*, I went to visit Daddy and did *kaparos* for him. His eyes were wide open and looking at me as I circled a cloth with *tzedaka* over his head. In the *Yom Kippur* service, there is a section with a very moving prayer where we say: "On *Rosh Hashana*, G-d writes what our fate will be for the coming New Year and on *Yom Kippur* it is sealed. Who shall live and who shall die." I couldn't hold back my tears.

The last days of *Sukkot* were arriving. As usual, I went to see Daddy after work. He was very alert and listened to me talking about the family. He hadn't been able to speak these past six weeks while on the ventilator because of the tube in his throat. I held his hand while I spoke. I told him *Simchat Torah* was in a couple of days. I said I wasn't sure if I would be able to visit for a couple of days, but would try. I couldn't promise. He squeezed my hand so hard it actually hurt. I couldn't believe it. I didn't pull away. Instead I said, "Good, Daddy! keep it up! I see you're squeezing my hand very hard. Keep it up, you're strong." He was looking right into my eyes with his bright blue eyes. Then he relaxed his grip, let go, and closed his eyes. I told him that I loved him. It was hard to understand how a ninety-six-year-old man could have such strength while on a breathing machine. Amazing.

Three days later, it was *Shabbos*. The volume on the answering machine was set on the loudest setting so that we could hear it anywhere in the house. We had explained to the hospital staff that we don't pick up the phone on *Shabbos*, but to leave a message and we will hear it. They seemed familiar with what we requested. The phone rang and we ran. It was the doctor: "I'm very sorry to tell you that your father has passed away." There is an expression about "knees buckling." I literally fell to my knees and bitterly cried out. Thank G-d, the kids were outside playing and didn't hear this kind of wailing. I knew this would come, but it's always a shock when it's final. I cried for a while and then asked Yaakov to bring the kids inside. I sat them down and told them their *zaidy* had died. They were naturally saddened by the news. Yaakov and I walked to the hospital to stay with Daddy until arrangements could be made after *Shabbos*. The children chose not to come along and stayed together at home. I asked the nurse to remove the tube and she cleaned Daddy up. We sat by his bedside, and I held his hand for the remainder of *Shabbos*. His hands were ice cold. I tried to warm them, but they just felt cold, like snow. Yaakov and I kissed his forehead; we needed to. We talked to him and told him how much we loved him. My father died in October 2003. He was ninety-six years old.

The following day was Sunday, and we had the *levaya*, the funeral, in my *shul*. This is where Daddy had *davened* with us weekly. Our rabbi emeritus and current rabbi had gotten to know Daddy well over the years. People in *shul*, both young and old, liked my father. It was time for me to do *kriah*, tearing the cloth of my shirt over my heart. The last time I had performed *kriah* was when my mother had passed away. Hershey and Magda, who had just visited Daddy less than two months ago, were now attending his funeral. It was especially hard for Hershey because my father was his last relative on the Gottesman side of the family from his childhood in Czechoslovakia. A few Rabbis spoke beautifully about my father and what a strong man he was. I'll never forget what our rabbi emeritus had said: "Mr. Gottesman sat in the back amongst the giants, but he was taller than all of us." What profound words. He made me smile. For Daddy to have gone through all he had and somehow to have come out intact and whole was incredible. My older son, Dovid, recited *tehillim*, and Yaakov spoke. He talked about the enjoyment our children had had with their *zaidy* and how proud he had been of them all. The children had brought him tremendous *nachas*.

Now it was my turn to speak. I went up to the pulpit and looked out at the audience for a few seconds. The room was packed! I knew that Daddy had been liked, but I guess I didn't realize what an impression he had made on others. I recapped my father's life from his happy childhood years through the end of his days.

My father, Morris Gottesman, would often introduce himself as Avrahom Moshe Gottesman and then would say, "Gottesman, *Ish E-lo-kim"* [man of G-d]. He was born in 1907 in Svalyava, Czechoslovakia. He was one of nine siblings. His father wore a *kaftan* and a *bekesha* on *Shabbos*. He told me his mother would go before *Pesach* to wash their dishes in a pond in the cold weather and the

Rabbi would tell her husband, "Tell Freida the dishes are *kosher.*"

My grandparents ran a grocery store in the back of their home, and my father would help out. Times were difficult. Influenza was rampant, and my father lost four siblings during that time. My father told me his mother would dip bread into whiskey and give it to the children to keep away the flu.

My father lost another brother who fought in World War I. He lost his parents and two more siblings during the Holocaust. My father's one remaining sibling Arieh passed away about twenty years ago. Arieh was survived by a daughter Nomi. My father also had a nephew Hershey who survived the camps. Nomi and Hershey are my two first cousins. My father was the only survivor of his large, immediate family. Along with other Jewish men, he had been taken by force by the Hungarian police, who were working under Nazi occupation. They were sent to the forced labor camps in Yugoslavia. He survived by his wits and sense of humor. When he talked about his experiences, it was with a sense of pride and an attitude of, "I survived, I won, and you couldn't kill me."

Although his formal education was only through eighth grade, he had a keen intellect. He knew nine languages, mostly of Eastern European origin. Every time a new regime took over, he was taught in that country's language.

After the war my father lived in Yugoslavia, and came to America in 1951. He met my mother through mutual friends, and they married in 1953. My parents were unable to have children for eleven years, but as my parents always told me, a miracle happened. My mother was close to forty-eight years old and my father was fifty-six years old when my mother gave birth to me. I would tell people my parents they were like Abraham and Sarah when they had me.

My father was a true businessman. He was quick, astute and knew how to *handel*, to bargain. When I was maybe three or four years old, my father owned a men's clothing store on Prospect Place in Brooklyn. His store had been burglarized. The criminal cut a vein on my father's neck and knocked out his teeth. Miraculously, he survived. We moved to Perth Amboy to be near my aunt and uncle. He continued to work in New York on Orchard Street on the Lower East Side. In the 1980s, shortly before I got married, he retired and sold our house.

In 1985, about the time Yaakov and I became engaged, Daddy moved to a new apartment complex in Perth Amboy adjacent to Raritan Bay, and one block away from the new *shul* that had been built after the fire. He lived there for the next thirteen years. Daddy missed his garden, so he asked the president of the *shul* if he could plant some tomatoes in the backyard. He was allowed, and shared the harvest with the *shul*. He had his daily routine: go to *shul* in the morning to *daven*, have breakfast, do errands, check on his investments, have lunch, take a nap, visit Aunty and Uncle, go back to *shul* for afternoon and evening prayers, dinner and bedtime, quite a full day for a retired man.

The one change to his routine that he welcomed was when I would bring the kids, usually once a week, to visit their *zaidy*, as they called him. He loved and cherished this time with his *eyniklach*, grandchildren. He would take them down to the water to look at the boats and walk on the pier. While they were visiting, *Zaidy* would squeeze fresh oranges on his juicer and serve the juice with cookies while the children watched TV.

I found my father's habits very interesting. When he counted money, he would always lick his fingers first. He didn't carry a wallet. The bills were folded over and when counting, he would unfold them towards himself and count in Yiddish. He was a fast walker. I would always have to walk quickly to catch up with this spry man.

When making *havdalah* (separation ceremony), there is a custom that my father followed from what he had observed in his parents' home while growing up. He would dip the tip of a finger from each hand into the ceremonial wine, and swipe them across the forehead to symbolize the hope that it would be a new and intellectually successful week. Then he again dipped a finger from each hand and put his hands in his pockets in symbolic hope of a financially successful week.

I concluded the eulogy with how he wound up in the hospital, his recuperation and move to my community where he lived happily for the next five years, and how he suffered from congestive heart failure, which ultimately led to his death.

At the end, my father needed to be put on a ventilator. He fought for six weeks and made it through the *Yomim Tovim*. He was unable to communicate through words, but he made eye contact and squeezed my hand. On *erev Yom Kippur* I did *kaparos* for him and he looked directly into my eyes. When I was done, he closed his eyes. He knew what was going on. Last week I told him *Simchat Torah* was coming and he began to cry. He was aware of what was going on. Every morning Yaakov saw him before going to work, and I saw him every day after work. This past

Thursday I was talking to him and saying *tehillim*. He squeezed my hand so hard it hurt, and he forced his eyes open to look at me. This was his goodbye.

At 1:40 on *Shabbos* afternoon, my father died. They say when someone dies on *Shabbos* this means he was a righteous person. My father loved going to *shul* and would *daven* constantly at home. He lived a hard life, but saw much happiness. He was so proud of the family I married into and he loved Yaakov. My father could not have been more blessed than to have a son-in-law like Yaakov. Yaakov has been an exemplary son to my father.

My father deeply adored his grandchildren, and they loved and respected him and gave him so much pleasure. I don't think my father ever imagined he would have had children, let alone meriting having grandchildren. He was blessed, and we and our children are blessed to have had him for as long as we did. He turned ninety-six years old this past August. He lived a long and full life, and now it is time for him to rest.

During the *shiva* for my father, his aide continued to help Aunty. She also helped pack up my father's belongings. Most of his clothes went to charity, but I kept certain items. Daddy always presented himself as a gentleman. He wore nice slacks, a button-down shirt and a jacket. On *Shabbos*, he would wear a handkerchief in the breast pocket of his suit. He also wore hats of different colors depending on the suit--gray, black or navy. Each hat had a small feather in the band. During the week, he wore a straw hat or a cap. He always looked put together, quite dapper. I saved two handkerchiefs with his monogram, and several hats. My son Asher was able to fit into one of my father's casual spring jackets. We put several pieces of my father's furniture into storage. It was a good thing that we did because even though it sat there for a while, we were able to give my newly married daughter a breakfront in very good condition and a headboard for their bedroom set. I told Rivki, "This is a gift from your *zaidy*."

(l to r) Yaakov, Rivki, Cecily Dobin, Dovid, Morris, Aaron Dobin, Miriam, Asher, Ella

Svalyava river, late fall or early spring, c. 1930

Svalyava Street after rain, c. 1930s

Svalyava City Hall, c. 1920 – 1930

DADDY

After Daddy died, I began going through his papers. I knew much of his family history, but needed to write it down. On my father's side, my *zaidy* was born in 1868, and my *bubby* in 1869. They owned a country grocery store and sold shoes, food, petroleum gasoline, women's scarves and so forth out of their house. They had a separate entrance for customers. They also owned five or six acres of farmland and were considered a middle-class family.

My father, Avrohom Moshe (Abraham Moses) Gottesman, was one of nine children. He was named after both of his grandfathers. He was born August 26, 1907, in Svalyava, Czechoslovakia. There were five boys and four girls in his family. Whenever my father talked about his family, he only used their Hebrew or Yiddish names. From the oldest to youngest, they were: Yitzchak, Yisrael, Sora, Rochel, Pearl, Avrohom Moshe, Arieh Leib, Leah and Nosson.

My father's family was Orthodox, but from a Chassidic background. The definition of a *Chassid* is one who is pious, and faithful, and tries to do more than is required by Jewish law. Chassidism originated in Europe in the 1700s with the great scholar and rabbi, the Ba'al Shem Tov, who was born in Podolia, Poland. He taught his students that as Jews, we should serve G-d through joy and fervent prayer. The Chassidim also wore their own special garb of white shirts and black pants and a *tallis katan,* a garment underneath the shirt with fringes attached on each of the four corners. On *Shabbos,* my *zaidy* wore a *kaftan* and a *bekesha,* a silk robe, and a *shtreimel* on his head. My *zaidy's* family were known as Belzer Chassidim. They had originated in Galicia, Poland, and come over the Carpathian Mountains after World War I.

My father grew up in Svalyava, a middle-sized town with a large Jewish community and some non-Jews. My father attended a big *shul* with a lot of people. He remembers that every *Shabbos* they would eat *shalosh seudos* with the rabbi of his *shul.*

It was a hard life. World War I began in 1914 when my father was seven years old. Men were being drafted for the army, and his oldest brother Yitzchak was taken to fight. The scourge of influenza was rampant. My *bubby* would give the children bread dipped in whiskey every morning as an antibiotic to ward off the influenza epidemic.

Sadly, in 1915 my grandparents received a letter that Yitzchak was missing in action. My father thinks it happened while Yitzchak was stationed in Italy. There wasn't even a body to send back for burial. So much tragedy and sadness engulfed the Gottesman family. Between 1904 through 1918, my *bubby* and *zaidy* buried four of their nine children. At age three-and-a-half, Rochel died of infantile enteritis (inflammation of the small intestine). Pearl at age ten, Leah, age six, and Nosson, age four, died of inflammation of the lung, also known as influenza. With the inventions of the Industrial Revolution came a modernity that touched the lives of many of the religious Jews of Europe. My father at age seventeen had his *payess*, sidecurls worn by Chassidic men, cut off by the barber. Afterwards he recalled, "I was so ashamed to go into the *Beis Medrash*."

My father shared some pleasant memories of his childhood with me. One of his favorite games was soccer, which they called football. At home, he helped his parents with whatever needed to be done in the house or their grocery store. Whenever he had free time, he would play with his friends.

Every morning he would wake up very early to go to *cheder* (religious school). After *cheder*, he walked three kilometers, round trip, approximately one-and-a-half miles, to go to grammar school. He attended school through eighth grade and had no further schooling past that. He learned nine languages in school because the borders kept changing with each new political regime. The majority of languages that he learned were Eastern European: Hungarian, Czechoslovakian, Slovak, German and Russian. He spoke Yiddish at home, and learned Hebrew in *cheder*. In America, he learned English and Spanish.

The school teacher was called Bertha *Neni* (aunt). My father told me that in the bitter cold winter after arriving at school, his fingers were frozen. Bertha *Neni* would rub snow on them to warm them up, and my father would cry because it hurt. A classroom could hold one hundred students, who were taught by just one teacher! If a student misbehaved, he was rapped on the knuckles by the teacher. In the afternoon, when school was over, Daddy would return to *cheder*. His *rabbaim* (plural of rabbi) were named Yerachmiel and Mordechai, but the students called them *Rebbe*, my teacher (an endearment).

I asked my father what his mother was like, and he said, "My mother was such a good woman. She was very religious. Before Pesach she would put little booties on the *ketzele's* feet not to bring the *chometz* in the house."

I asked him if he was serious and he laughed and replied, "No."

"And your father?" I asked.

"He was a good man, but very strict."

I recall my father saying this with a serious face. One day my father came home from *cheder* and told his father that his *rebbe* had given him a *potch*, a slap. My *zaidy* spoke to the rabbi, who told him not to teach him how to deal with his students. My father and his younger brother Arieh (Leiby) would playfully argue over who would get what they called, "Mamma's *challah*," special braided loaves of bread baked for *Shabbos*. Of course, Daddy always won because he was older. Daddy rode a scooter, sort of like a mini-motorcycle. I asked why and he said, "to show off." He also said he smoked cigarettes back then. I was surprised, but he said that it was nothing; it was also just to show off.

When I was a child and my father came home from work, I remember him walking through the front door, greeting me, and then going to the breakfront and taking out a bottle of schnapps. He did this every now and then. He poured some into a shot glass and drank it quickly, and then said, "Aah." It seems he needed this to settle him down after a long day. I know from his stories that it was common to have a drink on *Shabbos* after *shul*, both in Europe and here.

When Daddy was fourteen years old, his formal education ended. He started earning money selling bicycles. As the years went on, he also sold watches and anything else that he could sell-- whatever people needed. My father did well in business. He was well-liked and had a good sense of humor that he shared with his customers. Times were difficult.

In 1933, my father's brother Arieh moved to Prague before emigrating to Israel, which at the time was called Palestine. My father's brother Yisrael was married and had one child, Tzvi Hersh (Hershey). My father's sister Sora (Sarah) was also married. My father was single and still living at home.

Times were difficult. The countries around the world were still recovering from World War I. Adolf Hitler came to power in Germany in 1933. Many anti-Jewish laws were enacted in Germany and as news of these spread throughout the Jewish communities of Europe via radio and Jewish newspapers, people started to wonder if and how it would affect them. No one believed that this madman Hitler would be able to stay in power.

I was grocery shopping with my younger son Asher, who was nine or ten at the time, when I heard the couple in line behind us speaking Hungarian. The man said to his wife in a derogatory tone, *"szido"* (Jew). I can't express the anger that welled up inside of me. I looked at him and then at my son. How did he know we were Jews? Because my beautiful, young son was wearing his *yarmulke* on his head--*proudly*. Had I had the nerve, what I would have said, and should have said, "Yes, we are Jews, and proud of it!" Believe me, if my father had been there, the walls of the store would have shaken with his reaction.

I once asked Aunty how she had felt about having to wear the yellow star on her clothing, which had the word 'Jude' written on it as a form of identification and degradation for all to see. She said it didn't make her feel ashamed. She was proud of her Judaism. The Nazis tried to shame and degrade the Jews by forcing them to wear this outward symbol. It didn't work.

DADDY'S STORY

In 2000, my father dictated the following information to me so I could write down his story verbatim.

In 1939, I was thirty-two years old. At that time the Hungarians invaded Svalyava, Czechoslovakia, for the Germans. They advertised that all Jewish men under the age of forty should come work for the Hungarian army. The Hungarians were in allegiance with the Germans.

I went to Košice, Slovakia. They sent me with a company of Jewish men to work in the occupied territories [later known as "forced labor camps"]. There were different jobs I had to do. I worked in a vineyard, carrying stones to build a church, and helped build an airfield for the Hungarian Air Force.

Before we went to Yugoslavia, my company had one week to go back home. [*That was the last time my father ever saw his parents or remaining siblings.*] Then we had to report after the week to a ship to take us to Yugoslavia from a town called Erchi. The Hungarians then took us to Serbia, Yugoslavia. We dug a tunnel under a mountain. Along the mountainside, the Germans discovered that there was gold and copper at the bottom of the river, so the water should go through the tunnel to the other side.

While in this labor camp [*Bore, Yugoslavia*], there were eight young men who tried to run away to the Partisans and were caught. They were placed in a basement and were left there for months. They were given little food, but were kept there.

A new *commandant* [*captain*] came as a director for the camp. All the work units were brought out from the surrounding forced labor camps. The Hungarian military were all brought out as well. They were told by the new commander, "You can beat and hang up the boys by the hands, and if they are still alive, let [*take*] them down. When they regain consciousness, they will hang them back up."

At this time they brought out the eight Jewish boys and lined them up by a wall. Soldiers with machine guns shot them down to show everyone that whoever tries to run away will be shot down.

There were other jobs I had. My unit cut down trees in forests for cooking and heating. Now, I will again speak about the tunnel where gold was discovered in the river. While working in the tunnel, the gas from the bombing and all the materials from what was collapsing made me ill. The German foreman sent me to the '*kippa*.' I didn't know what the kippa was. My job then was to smooth over the material that came from the tunnel to cover the river in order for the river to dry out faster.

The Russians came from Romania through Yugoslavia. Then the Germans started retreating towards Hungary. When my unit was pulled out, we went towards Hungary. On the way, there was a ditch along the main street. My feet were injured, and my shoes were rubbing my feet until they were bleeding. I jumped into the ditch to escape. A friend and I did this. It was getting dark, and we remained in the ditch until the unit was out of sight. In the dark we saw a light up on a hill. My friend and I walked towards the hill. These events took place towards the end of the war.

There was a Serbian woman coming from the fields with a full wagon of vegetables. I spoke in Slovak to her and asked her for work and a place to sleep and eat. This woman and her husband put us up for several weeks. In the meantime, we got word that the unit that I escaped from was machine-gunned down. These people were very friendly to us and felt sorry for us. This was the first time in years that I sat at a table with chairs.

Daddy relayed this while crying many tears.

He told me that he had slept in this family's barn. My father had not davened in years. In the morning, he removed his shoe laces from his shoes and used them to wrap tefillin around his arm and around his head. The Serbian woman walked into the barn and saw this and alarmed she said, "Avrohom Moishku has gone crazy." Daddy laughed when telling me this story.

The Serbian man found work for me in his vineyard. The end of the war was approaching (spring 1945). I didn't hear anymore gunfire. I left this family and went to Belgrade [Yugoslavia]. I met up with other Jews from the Joint Distribution. The war was now over and I received word that my parents and siblings were murdered at Auschwitz. I stayed in Belgrade trying to make a living. I left to come to America in 1951.

I tried to use this information to help my father receive reparation from the German government. I had a wonderful German woman, a convert to Judaism, come meet my father. She took down his story and translated it into German. But the response we received was: "You are not of the German culture and therefore, denied." Ridiculous. It was just an excuse not to give him compensation.

My father never went back to his home in Svalyava because everyone had perished. He told me a horrifying story he heard from other Jews after the war. A group of Jews went into a general store. In the back of the store on a shelf they saw bars of soap with the name *Juden seif* – Jew soap. The Germans were diabolically ingenious. They thought of many uses for the Jewish lives which they destroyed: Shaved off hair was used to stuff mattresses, gold was stolen from tooth fillings, human skin was used to make lamp shades and after the bodies went through the crematorium where Jews were gassed, their bodies were burned in ovens and a certain amount of the ashes were manufactured into soap. This group took all the Jewish soap off the shelves, buried them and recited the mourner's *kaddish* over the dead.

Daddy stayed in Yugoslavia after the war ended in May 1945 until 1948, then moved to Germany and lived there until April 1951. He did well for himself as a businessman. He sold beautiful Rosenthal china sets. Two such sets he brought with him to the United States. He also had beautiful figurines that he proudly displayed on top of his breakfront. I believe that for him, these were symbols that represented survival, and that *he had won*--not the Nazi barbarians.

While going through all the papers that my family had saved for more than seventy years, I was so excited and enthralled to come across a treasure trove of old official documents and letters. I knew that my father had lived in Yugoslavia, but he had never spoken about having lived in Germany. This was a great find and added to the pieces of the puzzle of my father's life. I needed to find translators who could speak and read documents in German and Slovak. Amazingly, I found a German Jewish woman (whom I mentioned earlier) who lives in my community, and the nephew of an acquaintance of mine who is from Slovakia to translate these documents. The following three documents were my father's while living in Germany.

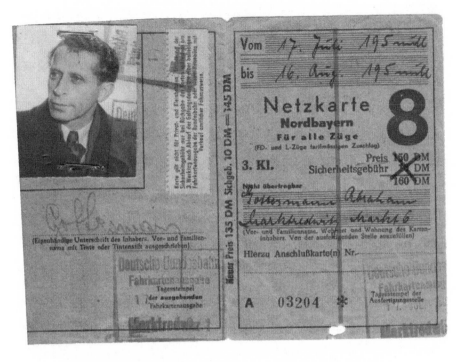

Train pass to buy for a certain amount to travel on any train. Train picked up from north Bavaria. Valid from July 17, 1950-August 16, 1950.

Signature: Gottesman, Abraham

Security fee of 145 DM in today's market. Travel went from the northern part of the southernmost state of Germany.

Marktredwitz--City in north Bavaria

Markt 6--Lived on Market Square #6

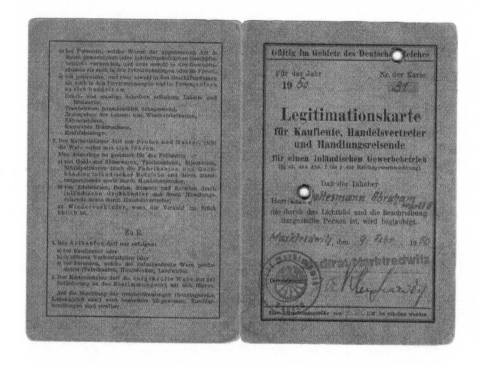

Legitimation Card for Merchants Card for the year 1950. Card assigned #31 issued at Marktredwitz, February 9, 1950. Salesman and traveling salesman for a company inside the country. Paragraphs of law that govern trade.

(Inside left)

Birthdate   26.8.07

Hair color   Dark blond

Eyes   Blue-gray

Body build   Small in stature

State belonging to   Stateless--Czechoslovakian Republic

Place of birth Svalyava formerly Czech Republic

Distinguishing marks None

(Inside right)

The holder of this card is entitled as an independent salesman to take orders of china (porcelain). He is responsible when receiving the orders (porcelain) for the payment.

German Identity Card (written in four languages: German, English, French, and Russian) – front & back covers

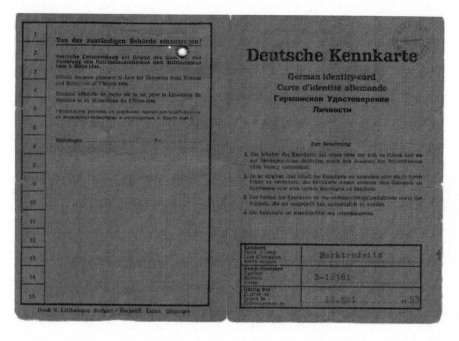

1. The holder of the identity card has to have it on himself at all times and be ready to show it to government officials or police officers upon request.
2. It is punishable by law to change the content of the identity card or to give it to someone else to use, or to use someone else's identity card.
3. Loss of card must be reported immediately to closest police station as well as to office that issued it.
4. The identity card is exclusively for use within Germany.

Place of issue   Marktredwitz
Number of card   B-12381
Expiration date   May 10, 1953

(Back Cover)(Not a translation)
If any individual belonged to the Nazi party or was involved in the military, there would be remarks in the open space and the identity card would be looked at more closely.

German Identity Card (cont'd) (written in four languages: German, English, French, and Russian) – inside

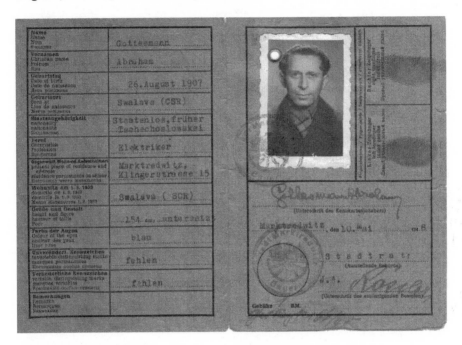

(Inside left)
Name: Gottesman
First: Abraham
Date of birth: August 26, 1907
Place of birth: Swalava (Czech Republic)
Nationality: Stateless, but formerly
                    a citizen of Czechoslovakia
Occupation: Electrician
Present place of residence and address   : Marktredwitz,
                                                            Klingerstrasse 15
Height and figure: 154 cm (5'4"), small in stature
Eye color: Blue
Invariable/variable: Missing
Distinguishing marks:

(Inside right)
Stamp for Marktredwitz, Bavaria
Fingerprints of Abraham Gottesman
Issue date of card–May 10, 1948
Fee for this card was 1 reichsmark
Stadtrat: Town Council

After discovering these official documents showing a German address, I couldn't understand why Daddy hadn't told me that he lived in Germany. The issue date on the German Identity card was from May of 1948. That means he lived in Germany for almost three years. A cousin of mine proposed a possible reason. Perhaps Daddy was embarrassed to say he lived in Germany because the Nazis and the German people were responsible for the almost total annihilation of the Jewish people, including his own family. After the war, Daddy never went back home to Svalyava because there was no one left alive from his family. He began a new life in Yugoslavia selling merchandise such as china. He told me how well he did for himself there. His plan was to come to the United States, but it took time. He needed to make a living and support himself until he could come to America and build a new life for himself. The reasoning that my cousin proposed makes sense, yet sadly I'll never know for sure. One thing is for sure, at least in my mind- Daddy never had to feel ashamed, he did nothing wrong.

One of the many lessons I've learned from having had parents who survived the Holocaust is that you should never judge that generation. Given the enormity of horrors they personally underwent and witnessed, it is impossible for others to understand their feelings and what they went through. I tell others that if, G-d forbid, another Holocaust were to happen today, there wouldn't be too many survivors. We don't comprehend the magnitude of how they suffered and yet, somehow, managed to go on living with all the losses they had experienced.

This is only a summary of my father's horrifying yet true experiences during this dreadful time in history. It never ceases to amaze me what a miracle man my father was. It never ceases to astound me how this man, my father, survived by his wit and wisdom, all while living in such fear, knowing that death could be near. He was very strong in spirit. G-d clearly wanted Daddy to live. It seems he was destined to accomplish much in his life. So many obstacles were put in my father's way and yet, by the true grace of G-d, he was able to survive.

IN THE MATTER OF THE APPLICATION   :
OF ABRAHAM GOTTESMAN FOR IMMIG-
RATION TO THE UNITED STATES UNDER   :
THE DISPLACED PERSONS ACT OF 1948

COMMONWEALTH OF PENNSYLVANIA   :
COUNTY OF BEAVER   : ss:
BOROUGH OF ALIQUIPPA   :

     I, FANNY HERSKOVITZ residing at 201 Fifth Avenue, Aliquippa, Pennsylvania, being duly sworn, depose and say:

     1. That I am a citizen of the United States.

     2. That I desire to sponsor the admission to the United States under the Displaced Persons Act of 1948, of ABRAHAM GOTTESMAN who is my first cousin and who resides at Markt Str. 6/II, Marktredwitz, Germany, U. S. Zone.

     3. That, if admitted to the United States:

     (a) the principal applicant will be employed as a clerk by Fanny Herskovitz at Aliquippa, Pennsylvania at not less than the prevailing rate of wages for like activity in the community where said employment will be pursued, and that the said activity will not displace some other person from employment;

     (b) the principal applicant will not become a public charge;

     (c) the principal applicant will have safe and sanitary housing at 201 Fifth Avenue, Aliquippa, Pennsylvania consisting of a room to be shared with my son without displacing some other person from such housing; and --

     (d) the principal applicant will be properly received by me or by someone in my behalf at the port of entry in the United States and the transportation and enroute expenses from such port to the place of destination shall be provided.

     4. That these representations and assurances are made by me in order that the above named ABRAHAM GOTTESMAN may be admitted to the United States under the Displaced Persons Act of 1948.

Fanny Herskovitz

Sworn to and subscribed before me
this 11th day of JAN. 1948

Daddy had a first cousin who lived in Pennsylvania. Her name was Fanny Herskovitz and she became his sponsor. He lived with her and her son before moving to New York. When Daddy arrived at Ellis Island, New York, he was doing what hundreds of thousands of other immigrants over many, many years had done: searching for a new home, a new life. Upon arrival, he decided he wanted a more American name. The man checking him in asked him why he wanted to change a name as beautiful as Avrohom Moshe [Abraham Moses]. My father said, "I want to be an American," to which the gentleman replied, "How about Morris? Welcome to America, Morris."

My father laughed as he told me this story.

Daddy went to night school to learn English. I remember him telling me that he had a good teacher. He demonstrated a sample of his lessons. The teacher took a piece of chalk, held it up and said, "Chalk." Then she put the chalk on the window sill, saying, "Now you know three words: chalk, window, and sill." He learned to read well, but unfortunately, never to spell well.

In 1952 Daddy met Mommy. They were introduced by mutual friends. They dated, became engaged, and married, all within six months. Both of my parents would laugh when they told me how Daddy proposed: "Would you consider marrying a short fellow like me?"

He was 5 feet tall and Mommy was five feet, four inches. Daddy would sometimes wear lifts in his shoes to appear taller. Even in pictures that were taken on the street, Daddy would stand on the curb while Mommy stood next to him on the street.

The actual date on their marriage license from City Hall is January 29, 1953, but they always celebrated their anniversary on February 1. [Perhaps] that was the date they considered their real wedding, when they were married under a *chuppah*, according to Jewish tradition.

Olga (Hecht) and Morris Gottesman

My parents settled in Brooklyn, where Daddy owned "Morris's General Dry Goods." It was a store that carried men's clothing, china, and bicycles. Mommy worked with him in the store. They both wanted to have children to bring new life into the world and replace all that they had lost. Mommy's menses had stopped during her time in the camps, and never returned. They sought help from many doctors, who put her on different medications. After nine years, Mommy became pregnant! She felt well and continued to work in the store. However, one day as she was climbing a ladder, Daddy saw some blood on the back of her dress. It was still early in the pregnancy and sadly, she miscarried. But they were very strong and determined people. Mommy desperately wanted a baby. They tried again. When I tell this story, I say, "They went from doctor to doctor, and then G-d sent them to the right doctor."

Two years later, Mommy became pregnant with me! Daddy told her that she shouldn't work any longer in the store, and she agreed. Thank G-d, she had a healthy pregnancy. I was born by caesarian section because the doctor didn't want to take any chances. Mommy was close to forty-eight years old, and hers was a high-risk pregnancy and delivery. I was born in 1964. My mother frequently told me, "The spring brought you to me." They were so happy. I was, thank G-d, a "miracle baby."

One of my cousins said that I looked like one of the Beatles, a very popular singing group at the time. I had thick, dark hair just like them. When I was six months old, my mother's doctors asked my parents to take me to the medical school so that the students could meet the 'miracle baby' they were learning about and my mother's specific situation. My father was very proud of this.

In 1965, my mother was diagnosed with a brain tumor. I'm sure there were several episodes leading up to this discovery including the one I mentioned earlier, when my mother literally stopped walking in the middle of a busy street in Brooklyn. The tumor was removed, but her recovery was not 100 percent successful. I was too young to remember, but without a doubt I'm sure Aunty and Uncle came to Brooklyn to take care of me and this way Daddy could tend to Mommy's needs.

The love and respect my mother shared with her sister Ella is something I witnessed repeatedly growing up. I never had a sibling with whom to share my thoughts and feelings. Their bond was indescribable. I know in my heart Mommy was at peace knowing that her sister picked up where unfortunately she had to leave off. I recently was thinking about the real possibility that one of the many reasons why Mommy wanted a child so badly was not just because she had this desperation to bare children after being barren for close to twenty years of her life. But she wanted to have a child to share with her dear sister, Ella who would never be able to conceive. It never ceases to amaze me how G-d caused these two wonderful women to share one child. There wasn't jealousy, just caring and concern. I was very blessed to have had these two mothers.

Olga, baby Miriam, Ella

AUNTY, MY SECOND MOTHER, AND LAST LINK FROM MY PAST

The year was 2003. Now that my mother, uncle, and father had moved on to *Gan Eden*, heaven, I turned my full attention to my Aunt Ella. I was so overwhelmed. I had a full-time job that I could not leave, and the kids were young and needed my attention. I didn't have enough time to devote to Aunty on a regular basis. Aunty's vision wasn't good any longer; she suffered from macular degeneration and could only see peripherally. The large-print books helped for a while and we got her books on tape, but she didn't have the patience for them. In general, it is a debilitating disease, but for Aunty, it was devastating because she could no longer read, which she loved, or sew, which was her livelihood and enjoyment for much of her life, or knit, which she also loved. I still have two lovely afghans she had made--one for her home, and one for my mother while she was in the hospital. She was trying to maintain as much independence as possible, but she couldn't deny that she needed help. I would do the weekly grocery shopping, pick up her medication, and take her to her doctor's appointments. I would visit her daily after work and get whatever she needed while doing my own errands. Lucky for me that the kids had a long day at school so I didn't feel like I was neglecting them.

The search for help began. Caregivers came and went--a few weeks here, a few months there. Eight women later, one of the aides recommended someone who spoke Hungarian. The women we hired needed to speak either English, Hungarian, or both. This was a must for Aunty, and I needed to be able to communicate with them as well. My Hungarian was not so great. My parents had spoken Hungarian with each other in the house, but to me they spoke only in English, so I understood Hungarian, but could only speak words or short phrases. This woman spoke both languages and her English improved as time went on. She had prior experience working with the elderly and those who suffered with dementia. She was absolutely wonderful. Her name was Esther--the same Hebrew name that Aunty had. Esther wasn't Jewish. No matter. Esther was extremely respectful of our ways and religion. She took excellent care of Aunty. She showered her daily, dressed her impeccably, fed her nutritiously, and went for walks with her daily. She would even put on Hungarian music and dance and sing with her in the living room. She had a great sense of humor and kept Aunty entertained, as well as all of us. She was with Aunty for the next fourteen months of her life.

In July 2010, Aunty became dehydrated and needed to go to the emergency room; Esther and I stayed with her. She remained in the hospital for five days, receiving much-needed fluids. During her stay I was afraid that this was the end, and while visiting her, I asked her for *mechila*, forgiveness, for anything and everything I had done that had hurt her during her life. If the opportunity presents itself, one should do this before a person dies. Aunty had been on several medications over the years to control her dementia. However, in the hospital the doctors had their own way of doing things and she had been taken off of the more potent drugs. I said, "Aunty, I need to ask you for *mechila*."

She looked directly at me, focused, and answered, "Not yet!"

Truly incredible. She was telling me that it wasn't her time yet. I looked at her, stunned, and laughed with joy. I knew she suffered from dementia, but during her hospital stay she seemed to have had several moments of lucidity.

The next day when I went to visit, her eyes were open and she appeared alert. When she saw me, she made eye contact and said, "I want to go home."

I said, "I understand, but the doctors are helping you because you were dehydrated, and you are looking much better now. It will be soon."

She seemed content with my explanation. I told her about the children and then, to distract her, I asked her how I should prepare the chicken soup for *Shabbos*. She had spoken very few words of late, and most of the time she was very quiet and couldn't always make eye contact.

She told me, "First, you put the chicken in the pot. Then, you add carrots."

"What about celery?"

"If you want. Then, you add water, but not too much."

I hadn't had such a conversation with her in months. She seemed to comprehend and process my questions and comments. The day she was to be released from the hospital I told her that we were taking her home, and she said, "I'm very happy."

I almost cried. She really understood.

In October 2010, Aunty had to go back to the hospital. This time the dehydration was more serious and, I believe, was related to what really had begun back in July. She had had difficulty keeping food down and needed to have a feeding tube put in. It was similar to Uncle's condition, but not as severe at this point. She was released after two weeks, and Esther--an absolute doll--was trained by a visiting nurse about how to feed her and keep the surgical wound clean. Her life continued pretty much the same way for the next few months.

In January 2011, Yaakov wanted to surprise me for our twenty-fifth wedding anniversary. Our anniversary wasn't until March, but that was only a few weeks before *Pesach*, and not a good time to go on vacation. We each set aside time in our work schedules and he surprised me with a cruise! It was a ten-day trip, departing from Florida, going to Puerto Rico and the surrounding islands. This was a real treat since we had never done something as extravagant as this before. Before we left, I left all the pertinent travel information with Esther and our kids.

We arrived in Florida on Thursday, January 13, and stayed in North Miami Beach by Yaakov's sister and family through *Shabbos*. Sarah, my sister-in-law, was to bring us to the port on Sunday. On Friday at 6 a.m., my cell phone rang, and it was Esther. Even while it was ringing, I had had a bad feeling. She was calling to say that an ambulance was on its way to take Aunty to the hospital. She had a fever and wasn't well. I told Esther that she had done the right thing and that I would call Dovid, my older son, to meet her at the hospital. I told Dovid where to find Aunty's information and her doctor's number, and that he was in charge until we could come home. I also called the doctor to explain the situation. We were on the phone back and forth for several hours with the doctors and my son. My younger son, Asher, happened to be in Florida for the year attending *yeshiva*, so he was visiting us, and it was comforting to have him there. My daughter, Rivki, was on winter break from college and was spending it in Israel for ten days and was expected back that coming Sunday.

The doctor said that Aunty was stable and he didn't think we needed to return. I still wasn't sure if that was the right thing to do, but we stayed for *Shabbos*. I was distracted, but it was *Shabbos*, and there was nothing I could do. When I spoke with the doctor after *Shabbos*, he said that Aunty's fever was due to a urinary tract infection, and that she had been put on an antibiotic. On Sunday, we were told that she hadn't responded to it quickly enough, because they had given her the wrong one, but that now, forty-eight hours later, she was on the correct one. We had begun looking into flights to return, but the doctor said that she was stable, and he didn't feel that we needed to return. However, since I had Aunty's Power of Attorney and was her next of kin, they needed my consent to put her on a ventilator. I gave my permission and Dovid took over a copy of the legal document.

Yaakov and I didn't know what to do. I was a nervous wreck, and felt terrible that Sarah and her family were involved, but they were wonderful. They said *tehillim* and the kids tried to cheer me up. For me, it was déjà vu all over again. When we were visiting Sarah several years earlier, my father had been having hallucinations, and his aide called in the middle of the night and threatened to walk out. I had to plead with her through bitter tears not to leave, saying we'd be home the next day.

Yaakov left the decision up to me and said he would be fine with whatever we did. He has always been a very supportive husband. Thank G-d, we've been married twenty six-years, and it's been quite a ride. Exactly half of our married life has revolved around the death of my mother and my uncle; my father's fall, recuperation and move to Highland Park; all of our issues with health care aides; Daddy's spending every other *Shabbos* with us and my children observing how to treat and be respectful of family; his last six weeks of life, and the period of *shiva*. Now, we were going through another upheaval with Aunty. Yaakov in all honesty has the patience of a *tzadik*, a righteous person. He could have thrown in the towel a long time ago, but as my children witnessed, you don't run away from problems--you learn to deal with them. That's what family is all about. Our children have observed the frustration, arguing, tension, tears, and laughter; the time spent with their *zaidy* and enjoying his company, and understanding from a young age that, in a family, it's not always rosy and perfect. You have to deal with the responsibilities in life that G-d gives you. You must never lose faith or hope. My children learned responsibility at a tender age, not unlike me, and they matured at a young age, not unlike me. As young adults, they take their responsibilities seriously, and have turned out to be content with their lives but still wanting to strive to do better. They, *baruch Hashem*, continue to mature and we are proud of each of them.

I spoke by phone with the nurse, who said that Aunty had been stable for a while, so we decided to go on the cruise. The ship was to leave in exactly thirty minutes. We received a call from the group coordinator who asked if everything was okay, and we said that we would explain when we arrived. I believe we were among the last to board. When we got to our state- room, there was a lovely lunch waiting for us. The cruise had a separate kitchen for the passengers who had ordered strictly *kosher*. What a wonderful start! We sat with a couple around our age at dinner, and enjoyed a show that evening. Monday at breakfast there was quite a spread: eggs, pancakes, French toast, mini-quiches, fresh fruit, cooked vegetables, lox, cheeses, fruit juice, and pastries. We sat with several people, mostly from New York or New Jersey. We saw a glass-blowing demonstration on the fourteenth floor of the ship, which was its highest point, and walked around getting to know what would be our new surroundings for the next nine days--or so we thought.

My cell phone rang during lunch. It was the doctor. Aunty's breathing was very shallow, and she could go into cardiac arrest at any time. Did they have permission to put her on life support? Can you imagine what kinds of decisions I needed to make--*again*? No one can unless, G-d forbid, he or she is in the same position. "You can't withhold air, water or nutrition from a person." The same words the rabbi had spoken about my father came back to me yet again. (We had been in touch with him, as well.) We wanted to do everything right by Aunty and needed to follow *halacha* to deal properly with life in such a fragile situation. I gave permission to put her on a ventilator. Yaakov looked at me and I said, "We have to go back." Yaakov agreed. I told the doctor we were docking tomorrow (Tuesday) in San Juan, and would be taking the first flight home. I spoke with Dovid and apprised him of our plans. He was amazing. At twenty-three, he was dealing with the doctors, Aunty's aide, visiting with Aunty to keep her company, and picking up Rivki from the airport. (We had spoken with Rivki and the two of them had gone right to the hospital upon her return the previous day.)

Once Aunty was on the ventilator, the kids called and I asked Rivki to put the phone to Aunty's ear. I told her that I loved her and I'd be there soon. Rivki said her eyes were open and she was listening. Aunty's rabbi and my rabbi told me some days later that Dovid and Rivki were wonderful. The way they both tended to their aunt's needs and dealt with the doctor and hospital staff was remarkable, and I should be very proud.

The cruise line staff was also remarkable. They allowed us to make a few ship-to-shore calls at no charge and offered to help in any way. When the ship docked, we were permitted to disembark first. The coordinators of the *kosher* group were sorry to see us go, but understood completely. A woman not connected to our group who overheard this conversation commented, "Why are you leaving? There really isn't anything you can do, and it's such a nice cruise."

Not that any of this was her business, but I explained that this woman was like a mother to me, and we needed to go home. Our *kosher* group coordinator said we were "very special people." It was a beautiful comment, but totally unnecessary. There was nothing to discuss.

Yaakov was completely fine with this. I kept apologizing to him that our trip had been ruined, but he insisted with a smile, and truly meant it, that whatever decision was made, it was the right one. He is an unusually positive person. He said that since nothing more could be done now, and we still had the rest of the day and evening, so we should enjoy ourselves, knowing that we made the right decision.

From the ship in Puerto Rico we took a cab to the airport and flew back to the Ft. Lauderdale airport. We were delayed close to six hours because there was snow back home in New Jersey. Someone on the staff said, "We're going to play a game." Anything to pass the time. He said, "If anyone has a penny that's older than 1931, they will win two free tickets to or from Orlando to anywhere in the continental U.S." Lots of "ooh's" and "aah's" were heard. Everyone started pulling out coins from their pockets. Guess who had a 1929 penny? Yep! Yaakov showed the coin to the staff member, and we were handed a pair of free tickets! G-d rewarded us.

Dovid picked us up from the airport at one o'clock in the morning and drove us directly to visit Aunty. It was very difficult to see her so helpless, and with a tube down her throat. The next day I spoke with the doctor and he said he would try to wean her off the ventilator, but that it might not work. They tried several times, but Aunty couldn't breathe independently for more than twelve hours at most, and that was with 40 percent oxygen being supplied.

Many new decisions had to be made. I was at the hospital daily after work. After about a month, Aunty had to be moved to a different facility that was better equipped for long-term respiratory care. The doctor moved the tube from her mouth to her throat by doing a tracheotomy. This reduced the risk of infection and would be more comfortable for Aunty. Unfortunately, because of this tube she could now no longer talk, but she listened and squeezed my hand.

Aunty then had a fever at one point and had to be transferred back to the hospital. We also had to start watching for bed sores. She needed to be turned from one side to the other several times daily. When she was stabilized, they returned her to the respiratory facility. This continued for over four months. During this time, I called my rabbi frequently. What unbelievable patience that man has! He was in contact with a relative of his who is both a rabbi and a biologist and answers difficult questions from around the world about protocol in Jewish medical ethics. I was at the point of begging my rabbi to say that we should let her go. I was afraid that she was suffering. The doctors all said that they were keeping her comfortable and that she shouldn't be in pain. I was a basket case. Thank G-d for my job! It was a healthy distraction for several hours a day. Another distraction was my daughter's love life.

About a week after returning from her winter break in Israel, mutual friends fixed her up with a nice boy named Azi (short for Azriel). As their relationship progressed, I would tell Aunty about it during my visits. At one point we thought the end was near for Aunty, and Rivki told Azi that she would like him to meet her. This was also just a few weeks before they became engaged.

By this time it was mid-April, and much had happened during the previous three months. We had said goodbye to Esther, our long – time home health aide. We knew that even if by some miracle Aunty was taken off the ventilator, she would need rehabilitation at a special facility and wouldn't be able to return to her apartment. There had also been water damage in her apartment. Luckily, insurance covered most of the repairs and with it, we eventually repainted the whole apartment, had new carpeting installed, and had a new kitchen put in. In reality, it was a brand-new apartment.

We had also celebrated Rivki and Azi's engagement with a lovely party in our backyard. Friends and family had come, and a date was chosen for the upcoming nuptials--July 12, 2011—a little less than three months away. Something gnawed at me about that date, and then I realized why: my father had fallen on July 12, 1998. It had also coincided that year with the Hebrew date of the seventeenth of *Tammuz*, which is a fast day. Thus it was a bitter-sweet date, but turned into a joyous date for our family.

One Friday afternoon late in May I was visiting Aunty and noticed that something was different, but I couldn't put my finger on what it was. I asked the respiratory therapist why she didn't have a tube attached to her throat and she said that Aunty was off of the ventilator. "What?!" was all that I could say. She showed me that the machine was gone. "When did this happen?" I asked.

"On Monday," she said, as she referred to her chart.

The doctor hadn't called to inform me. I began to cry tears of joy! I held Aunty's hand and she was squeezing mine hard. I told her that this was a real miracle. That a ninety-seven- year- old woman could wean herself off a respirator is incredible.

I said to G-d, "*Hashem*, what are you telling me?"

I kept talking to Aunty, and her eyes were clear and alert. She kept focusing on me and looking into my eyes while squeezing my hand. She still couldn't speak because the throat attachment had been kept in place in case the ventilator was needed again.

I repeatedly kissed her forehead amidst tears, and she looked at me through soft eyes. I called Yaakov with the great news and all he could say was, "*Wow!*"

It certainly was Wow! I then called each of the kids and my in-laws. I saw that Aunty was getting tired, so I kissed her, said "I love you," and left. I called the rabbi later with the good news and he said, "You see, Miriam."

I went to visit her the following week, but she was sleeping and I didn't want to disturb her. At 4:30 a.m. on Wednesday, June 2, the phone rang. A nurse said, "I am sorry to tell you, but your aunt has passed away. I checked on her and she was resting. Then a few moments later I came back, and she was gone. She wasn't in pain, and passed peacefully."

I know that *Hashem* had His reasons for detaching her from this machine ten days before her passing. I felt more at ease. We wouldn't have to make any more decisions regarding a Do Not Resuscitate (DNR) order. She passed peacefully, without a machine, and no heroics were involved.

Many people in my life who hear my family history think it's been such a burden and admire my devotion and dedication to my aunt. They don't get it. No one really can unless they have had such a close relationship with their aunt. In fact, while growing up and even to this day, I don't understand why so many people aren't closer with their parents' relatives. Yes, of course it was difficult, frustrating and annoying at times. The situation was far from perfect. Aunty used to apologize for being such a burden. I would say, "You are not a burden. I want to help take care of you." She and Uncle took care of me and raised me for most of my early life. My sister-in-law told me this is real *kibud av va-em*, honoring your mother and father. I guess what goes around, comes around. Our elders take care of us when we are young, and it is our duty and obligation to take care of them in their old age. It shouldn't be looked upon as being a burden, but as repaying a kindness. This brave and lovely woman raised me like I was her own child, and when she died, I felt as if I had lost my mother twice.

The evening before the funeral was her *tahara*. A group of women called the *Chevra Kadisha*, a group that cares for the dead, cleanses the body by carefully immersing the body in a *mikvah* (ritual bath), which brings a spiritual cleansing for the person's soul. After immersion, the body is dressed in a white shroud. Prayers are recited for the dead. The same procedure is done for men by men. This is a form of modesty and respect for the dead. I informed the *Chevra Kadisha* that I would like to have a few minutes alone with my aunt. I decided that I didn't want to see her face, and asked them to call me when she was fully covered. I didn't want to remember her that way. Her frame looked so small. She had never been large to begin with, but she had lost so much weight in the past several months. I said my goodbyes and asked for forgiveness.

Aunty's 89th birthday

AUNTY'S STORY

Arrangements were made, and the funeral took place on Friday. We flew Asher in from Florida. Azi, who was now part of the family, was naturally there, sitting beside Rivki. My family was all together. Aunty's rabbi and my rabbi spoke. Dovid and Azi recited some *tehillim*, Asher taped the eulogy, Yaakov spoke, and then it was my turn.

"To speak about my aunt Ella is very heartwarming and bittersweet. My parents are no longer alive, and my uncle is also gone. Aunty, as I always referred to her, was my last link to my past," I began.

As I spoke about Aunty, I recalled her happy childhood growing up in a loving home and traced her life until the very end. I chose to focus on her time during the war years in order to show how she persevered and survived this tragedy and loss and yet continued to live a long and full life.

Though Ella's story was being videotaped through the Shoah Foundation, I felt that as well-intentioned as the interviewer had been, she occasionally had cut into Aunty's monologue, and topics and thoughts were interrupted or omitted. So I chose to share Aunty's story as she dictated it to me in 1996, as well as through her Holocaust testimony on videotape and written information.

One day while Aunty was visiting, I took out a tape recorder and asked her questions that hadn't been explored during videotaping. Here are some excerpts from our conversation:

My name is Ella Reich. I got married in August of 1935 to Isadore Reich. We lived in Sečovce, Czechoslovakia. In 1938, Isadore was called to the army. Hungary took back parts of Slovakia, and my parents now lived on the border in Oborin and we lived in Hungary. When Isadore returned, [the] news was bad from Germany and what could be expected. We began to feel frightened in 1939. I cannot remember the exact date, but around 1940, radios were being confiscated. We had to wear a yellow armband on our sleeve. Later, they changed it to a Jewish star. In 1941, we learned that Jews were being persecuted by the Germans in Poland, and we expected the same thing to happen here, as well. Rumors began that the Germans would start to take the Slovak Jews away. There were anti-Jewish laws already enacted. In 1942, the Slovak Jews were being taken away. We knew we would have to leave our apartment and go into hiding. In February 1942, upon returning from work one day Isadore said, "Ella, we are leaving Galszecs [/galsij/]; we're going to Oborin."

We withdrew our money from the bank and took nothing else with us. We crossed the border and came to my parents' home. This was where my parents lived and where I grew up. They were surprised to see us because they didn't expect us. We stayed only for a day. It was a border town, and we would be noticed.

The family had learned through newspapers and by word of mouth what Hitler was doing in Europe. All had hoped that the war would be over before the Nazis entered Hungary. The Hungarian Jews were the last to be taken.

The Hecht family hid valuables, hoping to come back one day. They buried jewelry, such as Aunt Ella's engagement ring.

Aunty also had brass candlesticks that her mother-in-law had given her as a wedding present, and intricate needlepoints that she had made. These were some of the items that were given to their neighbors for safekeeping. Aunty was married by then, and she and Uncle had been in hiding since 1942.

After the war, when Mommy and Aunty went back to the Hecht home, Mommy found everything where they had left it, and the neighbors, who liked the Hechts very much, returned what they had been given to safeguard. The irony is that, sixty years after the war, when Aunty was suffering from dementia, one of her home health aides stole her engagement ring at about the time she gave notice. Aunty had told me years ago that she wanted Dovid, her oldest great-nephew, to give this ring to his kallah when he got engaged.

Then we went to Király-Helmec [Hungary] where my sister, Olga lived with her husband. We stayed with her a few days.

We had to move around because people would recognize strangers. We moved around Hungary so as not to be noticed because we were strangers and people would be suspicious. We moved around every few months. Isadore got a message from his boss that he had a permit to keep working in the textile store where he worked before we ran away. I stayed by my sister's home. A couple of months later, I got a message that Isadore [was] going to Miskolc, Hungary, and that I should meet him there. Then our wandering began. It's difficult to express the fear I felt to travel. I had an uncle living there and Isadore's boss's daughter lived there, too, and she helped us. I stayed with the daughter and Isadore stayed elsewhere. We were afraid to be seen together because strangers were noticeable. My husband, Isadore Reich, was called over to City Hall. He was called a second time, but he was afraid of being put in jail or a labor camp if he had gone back, so we left for Budapest. We got false papers and were able to travel to Budapest. We stayed with two cousins in an apartment and they found us an apartment to rent. My husband was looking for work because men [of] his age couldn't just loaf around the streets; he had to work. I looked for work, too. I knew how to sew, so I worked for a seamstress just to be out of the apartment (during the day) where we lived. We were registered to receive food tickets, but were afraid to claim them. Isadore was thirty-three at the time and I was almost thirty.

We went back to Király-Helmec. We heard that another cousin of ours from Slovakia had been caught while hiding. We received a note from a cousin that the man who gave us the false papers [had] reported them. The note said, 'The cheese is spoiled, get rid of it.' It was good that we left Budapest. Then we went to Iloncza. We stayed by Isadore's sister. Then we moved to Nagyszöllös. We always stayed with Jewish people. We always had a connection. We had to keep moving. Very often there were raids, and we had to go out from the house or the apartment where we were hiding because raids were common, and the police were on the lookout for strangers in houses. We arrived by a friend of Isadore who use to work in Galszecs with him. They didn't know that we were coming. So we opened the gate and went to the stable (because they had horses), and we climbed up to the loft and were hiding there until morning. The man's father came to feed the animals, and Isadore called out to let him know we were there because he was scared. We explained what was happening. He gave us something to drink and then we returned to the place where we were living.

We went to another place to live in the same town where we were hiding; always by Jewish people we were hiding. It was pretty nice there. The husband was in a forced labor camp and there were three boys with the mother. Once the mother was away visiting her mother, and we were sleeping in one room and the boys were in another. One night we had to run out from the house. One of the boys came knocking on the door: "You have to go away because they were just knocking on the window. They want to open the gate; they want to come to see if there are any strangers in the house." Now you could imagine the feeling. So we got up and put something on ourselves and ran out from the house, and the boys covered our being there. They put everything under the bed; the bed they threw over so it looked just like the three of them were there. We had to run over a high fence. I don't know how we jumped over. There were fields and we were hiding in a ditch for the night and all the next day. It was summer.

Towards the evening, the boy who lived in the house called out in a little Hungarian song, "You can come out, your house is safe."

So we climbed over the fence again, but a Gentile neighbor noticed us and ran into the house to tell his wife that he was going to call the police.

"What for?" she asked.

He said, "There are strangers in the Willinger's house."

She said, "You are not calling the police. I know of them, they are nice people. They are hiding here. They are running for their lives."

He didn't go to the police. We stayed for a while, but we didn't feel safe much longer there so we left. We found another place to stay in the same city. This happened during 1943.

Then we lived almost two years in Nagyszöllös. We stayed by a very religious family. It was nice there. We paid them for the room and what they fed us. My husband never went to the city. I did go out because a woman wasn't so noticeable, and I speak Hungarian. It was '44. Already they were taking the Jewish people from Hungary and I guess my parents were taken already, too. I don't know when or how. The Nazis established a ghetto in Sollos. This is where Isadore and I were already living. They took the prominent people from the city to City Hall, and they were investigating and asking lots of questions and sometimes beating them up, too. So my husband somehow managed that we should walk into the ghetto willingly to avoid the beating. It was April 1944, the second day of Passover, when we went to the ghetto.

We were in hiding for two-and-a-half years. We already lived in the area where the ghetto was established, so we literally walked into the ghetto by ourselves. We were not registered, and Isadore was afraid we would get beaten if we went down to City Hall. Isadore had an idea. He approached an officer outside the gate and said, "We were already in the ghetto, but they let us go home to get clothes. Would you take us back into the ghetto?" We saved ourselves from trouble. We were in the ghetto from second day [of] Passover until beginning June, after the holiday of Shavuot. They started to empty the ghetto; two transports left. We were the third transport from the ghetto going to Auschwitz. I took some dresses, but it was taken away. [*A gentleman well versed in this period of history explained the sequence of events to me. How the Jews were rounded up was very organized. The Germans selected a gathering place near railroad tracks. They then put people on wagons who were from small areas where they set up a ghetto. They made a sweep of the small villages and kept them in the ghetto area. When the time came to transfer the Jews to the concentration camps they would put them on the mainline which went directly to the camps.*]

I just can't describe the feeling. They pushed us on the cattle cars; we were pressed so many people together. It's just unbelievable. . . When I think about it, it seems like it's impossible. While on the cattle trains, we heard that people were being gassed already in the wagons and came dead to camp. We heard the wheels. I tried to sleep, but couldn't sleep. I had no idea how much time went by. We arrived in Auschwitz. As we got off the train we heard, "Out, out, out!" (Later, I met a cousin of mine who came in on a different transport. She had a baby about a year old. There were Polish *Kapos* there. She told me one was grabbing the child away from her. She said, "Don't take him!" He said, "Then you will die, too." He took the baby.)

The men and women were separated. Those told to go to the left were never seen again. Then I saw Dr. Mengele. He asked me if I was willing to work. Surely I said, "Yes." So I went to the right. My husband told me, "Whatever they ask, if I want to work, I should work." I went to a building to take a shower. My hair was cut off completely, so we shouldn't get lice. I was given somebody else's clothes and I had my own shoes. We came to the gate, went through and saw barracks. There were about thirty barracks. We were marching and marching and marching. I heard my name; Ella Reich, Ella Hecht. A second cousin of mine, Ilush Roth, pulled me out of line. She said, "Your mother and sisters are here." They knew from Sollos there was a transport that day so they were watching out for me. I was happy to be with my family. I was in the same barracks with my mother and three sisters. We slept five across and five long. There were three levels, ten people on each, feet to feet. I knew my father and two brothers were somewhere. When speaking with my mother while we were in Auschwitz, she told me that after she visited me last in *Nagyszöllös*, while on the train returning home to Oborin, right from the train the German soldiers removed all the Jews and put them in the ghetto in Ungwar (Uzhhorod, Hungary) even before they officially started rounding up the Hungarian Jews.

This meant that Ella's mother wasn't home when the Hecht family was rounded up and brought to the ghetto. Her father had no idea what happened to his wife.

Then started life in Auschwitz concentration camp; all kinds of stories, and the hidings and the scares. There wasn't much to eat. They gave us some soup. It seemed like there was sand in it. Maybe some meat. The girls in charge of the barracks would give out food, and they would look through and take out the meat. Work we didn't do; it was miserable. My sister, Roze, said to me she won't be able to eat this. I told her she must eat whatever they give us. We were given bread in the morning.

One night it was raining, and there was a big hole that was filling up with water. We were given buckets to clean it out so there shouldn't be any sickness. We would pass the full buckets down a line of women to empty the water.

There was an *appel* every morning. We got up early, stayed in line, counting. When there was a selection, me and my sister, Olga, ran to another barrack. We would stand five in a row. We knew a selection was happening. It came Yom Kippur and we were fasting. They gave us bread for breakfast, and we saved it for the evening so when the fast was over we would have what to eat. It was a Wednesday that year, Yom Kippur. Thursday was selection for our barrack, number 31. Olga and I stood in the row behind my mother and two other sisters. We didn't see what was going on in the row before us, but when we went to the barracks, Mengele was there. We saw our mother and two sisters go to the left. We went further in. They were selected and went to another barracks. It was the day after Yom Kippur. We never saw them again; they were killed two days later.

I once saw a wagon brought into our camp and it was full of bodies; dead bodies packed like they would pack wood used for heating a home. They were naked. They were placed like wood: crisscross, piled up. They were put in some barracks. Never before or after did I see this again.

We were moved across to another barrack, number 28. We met a girl there who knew one of my sisters. She told us that my mother and two sisters had been gassed. So I knew I would never see them ever again.

I asked Aunty what they had done with the people who had been gassed. She told me, "I learned about the showers where they would gas people and put them in the crematoria. The ovens weren't far, it was right there in Auschwitz. We saw the flames; we smelled the flesh and we saw the smoke, and we knew what was going on. When Isadore and I came to Perth Amboy, New Jersey, to live, there are lots of oil refineries. When I saw the smoke coming from there--that's what it looked like in Auschwitz."

My sister, Olga, and I were selected to go to work. First, we were taken to a real shower because we were going away. At first, we didn't know if it was to take a shower or to take gas. We were taken by open cattle trains. In October 1944 we went to Nuremberg. It was like a new camp. We got a room with a stove in it. The barracks were like small houses. The beds were on two levels and two in a bed. I stayed with my sister. We received meals. We hadn't been there too long and bombs were falling from American or English planes, so we already knew what was going on. We had to run to the shelters. I think it was January when they took us to work. We were taken into the city of Nuremberg to a factory in a streetcar. There were women guards. We were wiring wheels for airplanes. We received a decent meal. This was once. Then again we were taken to work, and then came the air raids. Bombs hit the building we were in, but we were in the basement, so we were alright. But we were stuck there. The door was jammed by debris. We had to dig our way out and walk back to Nuremberg where the camp was. The streetcars were ruined; it was a mess in the city, but it was good to see. The little houses were ruined, too, everything flat. Bombs were still coming, so we went to a shelter and when we came out everything was bombed and gone. One bunker was hit by the entrance and a German was killed and the guards were angry. "Why a German, why not a Jew was killed?"

We stayed there just a few days because they had to bring in the food, so they took us into the city of Nuremberg. We were in a building where there was water and it was dark and we were sleeping there a few nights. I don't know what it was: a restaurant, tables in the room and we were sleeping on it, if you call that sleeping. They gave us something to eat. Finally, they took us away because it was impossible to stay there. They divided us into two groups; there were a few hundred of us women. Then we were put on a train to Holýšov in Czechoslovakia. It was a small farming town. It was close to Pruzen. We stayed in a place that was like a farm; it had stables. Again, we were sleeping in bunk beds. Two rows and two in a bed and there weren't too many SS guards so it looked like it would be alright. They didn't punish us; no counting us. We would pick and store potatoes like we did back in my parents' home for the winter. We went to work in a munitions factory. We put gunpowder into shells and stamped it. Once, when I was pouring the powder into a shell, I cut my finger and it became infected. My hand swelled up. When we got back to the farm, my sister boiled potatoes in water, and I put it on my hand and the swelling burst open. It would heal. Today I have a scar from it. We went to this factory maybe three times and then that was bombed out. This was in the spring of 1945.

We heard help is near. We just prayed that they should reach us alive. One day we didn't see any guards. Then the Partisans came [May 5, 1945]. We were on the outskirts of Holýšov and they took us into Holýšov.

In an article entitled Freedom at Holýšov, author Ruth Cohen, also a survivor of Auschwitz, Nuremberg and Holýšov, explains that the Partisans did come in on May 5, but they kept the women locked in Holýšov for fear that the German people outside the camp would come in and bother the women. The Partisans told the women that the Americans were nearby and on May 7, 1945, the Americans liberated Holýšov. After speaking with her, it's probable that she was in the same places at the same time with Mommy and Aunty.

I really don't know if they were Russian, Poles, or Slovaks--probably Czechs because we were in Czechoslovakia. We had to walk into town. The next day, the American army came in. Trucks of American soldiers threw chocolates. This was really the end of the war. We were happy to be alive. Bread was given to feed us. Every day we went to eat a good meal in the village. We were happy to find people alive. They deloused our clothing. We showered and were fed well. We stayed there for four weeks. My sister, Olga, would go with other girls to see what was happening. Then they started to organize who wanted to go where. After four weeks Olga and I said we wanted to go home to Galszecs *(Sečovce is its equivalent in Hungarian)*.

They took us first to Prague. Olga was married, but her husband had been taken away to forced labor at the end of 1942 and she hadn't heard from him since then. People were very nice in Prague. They asked what we needed. We received food tickets and were given Hungarian money to go home. There were lots of Russian soldiers, too. From there we got organized again and took a train to Brno. They put us on trains to Morava which was then in Czechoslovakia and then onto Bratislava [which is now the capital of Slovakia]. There, they didn't even let us into the waiting room. They chased us out. This was now the end of June 1945. We had to stay in the hot sun, and there were people milling around the city inquiring of each other who is who and from where, in order to make a connection to lost loved ones. Someone recognized me and said, "I know you." I knew him, too. He was a banker In Galszecs. He said, "You know, your husband is home in Galszecs." I was very happy! He said Isadore's boss is here in Pressburg (Bratislava), and in which hotel they are in. We went to see them, but they had already left. Then we went to Budapest, Hungary, in an open train. Different Jewish organizations were waiting for us and took us in. We got clean clothes, beds, food, and we stayed for a while. We had to find a way to get home. In many places the tracks were taken off, so we had to find another place to get on a train. My sister and I stayed together throughout. Then we arrived in Kassa (Ku/sha), and we found the people that my husband was working for, the Wintners. They were very nice and very helpful. We stayed by one of their sons for *Shabbos*, and surely they let my husband know that we were here. On Sunday, Isadore came for us. I was miraculously reunited with my husband.

We went home on a horse-driven carriage because we didn't have buses right away after the war. He was living in the Wintners' house. They were old people. He told me the story that when he came home they were feeding him, he was so weak. My sister didn't find her husband and heard he died in the camp. My father and two brothers died, too. Isadore's full family was killed. Everyone was gone.

We started to get organized and find an apartment. We first went to Oborin to my parents' house. We spoke with the neighbors, who kept the clothing and furniture and valuables from my family in case someone came back. They did return these possessions. After returning home, then Olga went with Isadore to Király-Helmec, where she used to live with her husband, and found her furniture and belongings and brought it back.

The Wintner family looked at Isadore like a son. They were very good to him, but he was very good to them, as well. He was a real, real good guy. They said, "Isadore, here is some money. Go on the bandwagon and go make a living." Their store was empty because their sons opened another business in Kassa. They were selling wholesale in textiles. Isadore was with them for many years when we got married, and he was making a living and learned the business. He bought merchandise, and we opened up a textile store. We made a good living. He took in a partner because it was easier. One would go shopping, one had to be in the store.

We didn't intend to stay there; we couldn't. We had relatives in America. Isadore wrote to his cousins and they sent us some money. He wrote them to please not send us money or packages, but to send us papers so we could emigrate to America and papers for Ella's sister, too. That's what they did. They sent us papers, then tickets.

We had to wait a long time after applying for a visa to receive it to come to America, because there was a quota. This was in 1945. We had passports to go to Uruguay, Paraguay, but we waited for American visas.

Finally, on December 31, 1948, we crossed the border from Czechoslovakia into Poland. We went to the harbor of Odraport. On New Year's Day, January 1, 1949, we took a ship to Sweden. We were there about five or six days. From there, we boarded the Gripsholm [a Swedish-American line] that came to Canada, and from there to the United States. For eleven days we'd been on the seas. We (Isadore, me, and my sister, Olga) arrived in New York Harbor.

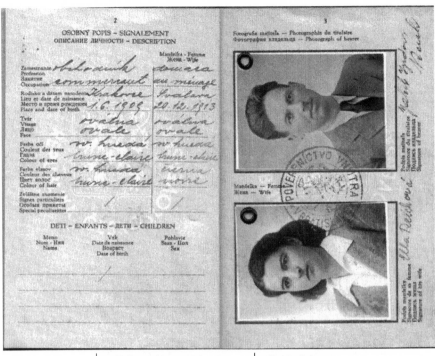

	Jakub Izidor Reich	Ella Reichova
Occupation:	Salesman	Housewife
Birth:	Krakovce, June 1, 1909	Svalava, December 20, 1913
Face:	Oval	Oval
Eye color:	Light brown	Light brown
Hair:	Light brown	Black

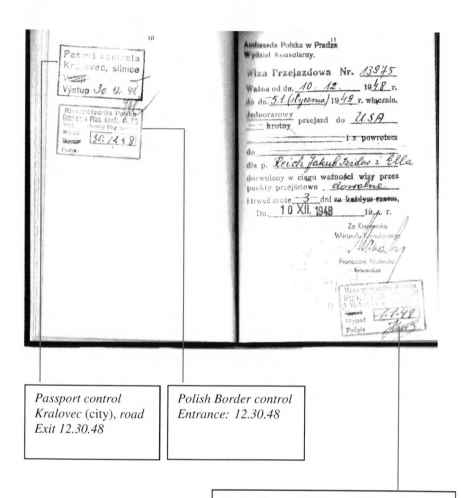

Passport control
Kralovec (city), *road*
Exit 12.30.48

Polish Border control
Entrance: 12.30.48

Stamp from Polish embassy in Prague,
which allowed Reich Jakub to leave from
Czechoslovakia through Poland for USA
from 12.10.48 to 1.5. 1949

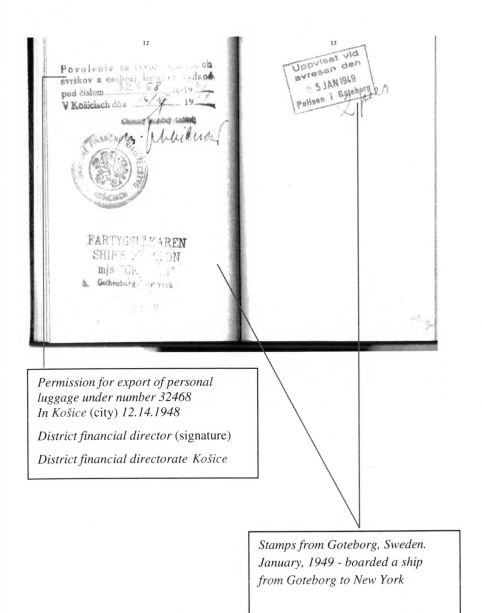

Permission for export of personal
luggage under number 32468
In Košice (city) 12.14.1948

District financial director (signature)

District financial directorate Košice

Stamps from Goteborg, Sweden.
January, 1949 - boarded a ship
from Goteborg to New York

Kôpt av
Salt till passinnehavaren
£ Shr 70 hr 1.000 (thus.)
Göteborg 5/1-49
SKANDINAVISKA BANKEN
AKTIEBOLAG

823054

POUCENIE

Ceskoslovenskí občania smú prekročiť hranice Ceskoslovenskej republiky, cestovať a zdržovať sa v cudzine len na základe platného cestovného pasu, ktorý podľa predpisov štátu, do ktorého cestujú alebo v ktorom sa zdržujú, musí byť opatrený vstupným alebo pobytovým povolením (vízom).

Majiteľ cestovného pasu nesmie v ňom prevádzať žiadne zmeny alebo doplnky. Takéto konanie malo by za následok stratu platnosti pasu a bolo by trestné.

Pre každú osobu má byť vydaný samostatný cestovný pas, avšak manželka môže byť zapísaná v cestovnom pase manželovom a deti mladšie 15 rokov môžu byť zapísané v cestovnom pase rodičov, s ktorými cestujú. Keď je manželka zapísaná v cestovnom pase svojho manžela, nemôže použiť k samostatnej ceste tento spoločný pas a je povinná opatriť si cestovný pas, znejúci len na jej osobu. V danom prípade je zo spoločného cestovného pasu vypísaná. Keď dovŕšia deti, zapísané v cestovnom pase rodičov, vek 15 rokov, musí byť pre ne opatrený cestovný pas samostatný.

K zamestnaniu v cudzine pravidelne treba zvláštneho povolenia úradu štátu, v ktorom má byť zamestnanie nastúpené. V zahraničných štátoch platia rôzne ustanovenia o policajnom hlásení k pobytu a rôzne predpisy o povolení pobytu. Presné poučenie o týchto predpisoch možno obdržať u miestne príslušného československého zastupiteľského úradu.

Pamätaj vždy, že každé tvoje konanie a správanie sa musí slúžiť ku cti štátu a národa, ktorého si príslušníkom.

421746

Stamp from National Czechoslovak Bank in
Prague, date 12.27.1948
Amount 70

Instructions:
Czechoslovak citizens can cross borders only with valid passport and required traveling visa.
Owner of the passport can't change anything in the passport. This is illegal and punishable.
Wife and children younger than 15 years could be added in husband's passport but if she travels alone, she needs her own passport.
For work abroad you need to have permission of the visiting state. Every state has own regulations. Exact text of regulations you can get at Czechoslovak consulates.
Always remember that your behavior must serve your nation and state dignity, to which you belong.

My uncle and Isadore's uncle and cousins were waiting for us and we came to them in Newark, New Jersey. From Newark, we went to Pennsylvania to my mother's brother. The three of us stayed there for two weeks. Then Isadore and I went to Pittsburgh, Pennsylvania, where we rented an apartment and we started to look for work. Soon after, Olga came to join us.

I had a first cousin from Europe who came in 1946. His name was Hugo Princz. He was a naturalized citizen through his father, who had come to America many years earlier, before returning to Europe. In 1949, Isadore and Hugo came down to Perth Amboy, New Jersey. Isadore had some relatives in the area, and he and Hugo decided to open a business there together. They bought a grocery store. Then Olga and I came down to Perth Amboy, and we rented an apartment, and we started a living. As things go, Isadore didn't stay too long in this business and had to give it up. Isadore and Hugo went their own ways, but amicably. They were cousins through marriage and we all stayed close throughout the years.

We went to night school to learn the English language and in 1954 we became United States citizens. Isadore found a good job in Two Guys, a department store in Woodbridge, New Jersey, where he became the manager of the fabric department. He was happy there because the work was similar to the work he had done in Europe. I knew how to sew, so we opened up a small dress shop, and so we started a living. We were feeling free. We were happy here in America. We had freedom, we made a nice living. As long as I was in Auschwitz I knew what was coming, and we expected every day it will be finished with us. But I was always praying that G-d should give me life, I should see how the world will look after this horrible thing. But it doesn't look too promising in my eyes what is going on again. We could never get over what happened. It has never left us. We lived together almost sixty years, married happily. No children. He just passed away. He would have been eighty-six years old on June 1.

If you wish to hear Aunty's story in *her* own voice, please go to www.lambecauseofyou.net.

When I was ten years old I came home from school to find my mother and aunt in the kitchen. My mother had suffered a stroke and they were waiting for the ambulance. My father was on his way home from the Lower East Side, where he worked. My father had to work, so who would take care of a ten-year-old child? Without a thought or question, my aunt and uncle moved me into their home and raised me as their own. I spoke with my father daily and spent *Shabbos* with him. My aunt cooked for my father for the next fourteen years while my mother was in the hospital. Our Sunday afternoons were spent visiting my mother.

Aunty and I had a very special relationship. She was truly a mother to me. We argued like mother and daughter, I confided in her all my thoughts, and we loved each other like mother and daughter. She bought me dolls, sewed clothes for them, made me vests, skirts, and Purim costumes. Aunty was a very talented and skilled seamstress. She owned her own dress shop, called Ella's Dress Shop, in Perth Amboy for twenty-eight years.

Aunty and Uncle lived a modest life because that was the way they chose to live. They instilled values and ethics in me that Yaakov and I have tried to impart to our own children: to be an honest and genuine person and to treat others with respect is the ultimate *mensch*.

When I began dating I brought home a boy from a background similar to Aunty's. When she saw what he was like, I asked what she thought. She said, "He's not for you."

"You're right," I replied, "but why?"

She said, "You don't need someone whose parents went through what we did, you need someone fun."

When Yaakov met my family, they liked him right away. They saw a good and kind person, and they were very happy when we married. The greatest joy for Aunty and Uncle and my parents were Dovid, Rivki, and Asher. Dovid is named after my mother's and aunt's father, and Rivki is named after my mother.

In 1995, my uncle died and I watched Aunty grow old quickly. They were each other's life. They were married almost sixty years. We moved Aunty to Highland Park that year, where she lived happily for over fifteen years. She made many friends and enjoyed coming to *shul* here weekly. In 1996 she was videotaped by a representative from the Spielberg Shoah Foundation, and her story will be passed down as a legacy for our children and their future families. Aunty loved to read, knit, and crochet, so when she was struck with macular degeneration, it began to shake her confidence. She continued to live as independently as she could. She began shopping with a B*ikur Cholim* volunteer, and began to form new friendships. Around seven years ago she began showing signs of dementia. Within two years she could no longer live alone, and we got her a full-time aide. Over the course of time, she stayed strong and was lucid much of the time.

In January [of 2011] she went to the hospital because of an infection. Yaakov and I were away celebrating our twenty-fifth wedding anniversary. Dovid took charge while we were away. We received a call from the doctor that her pressure was dropping, and a decision had to be made. She needed to be put on a ventilator, and we flew back home. Over the next four-and-a-half months, Aunt Ella would fight to survive. She was a very strong woman.

Throughout all this, life continued, and our daughter, Rivki, brought a healthy distraction to our family. As many of you know, Rivki is engaged to a wonderful boy, Azi. Whenever we visited Aunty, and if she was lucid, we would share with her all the news of Rivki's courtship and engagement. It meant a lot to us all that Aunty was able to meet Azi.

When *davening*, I always asked *Hashem* to have mercy and give comfort to Aunty, and that she should not be in pain. On May 23, a miracle happened: She no longer needed the ventilator. She was breathing all on her own, with some oxygen to help. However, she had had a tracheotomy tube in her throat while on the ventilator, so she couldn't speak. When I saw her off the ventilator, I kept kissing her forehead and crying, and her eyes were open and focused on me for more than twenty minutes. I had not seen her so alert in quite a while. She held my hand with strength and listened attentively as I spoke about all that was going on in the family. June

1ˢᵗ was my uncle's birthday. Soon after, Aunt Ella died and went to join him again. She died peacefully.

The last *chesed* (kindness) I could do for her was say the *mechila* prayer for forgiveness after the *tahara* that last night. This woman was truly a second mother to me. I feel as if I've lost my mother twice. What I will always remember about Aunty is her strength, her perseverance, and her smile for her family, which showed how deeply she loved us all."

The day of Aunty's funeral was so strange. Since Aunty and Uncle didn't have children of their own, sadly, there was no one to sit *shiva* for her. I spoke with my rabbi and explained that this woman had been more like a mother to me, and a grandmother to my children. I not only wanted, but needed, to sit *shiva* for her; this was the last kindness I could do for her. It wouldn't be the regular *shiva* where you sit and mourn for a week. I explained to the rabbi that it was the least I could do for her, even if just for a few hours. He agreed.

I received at least twenty-five visitors that afternoon, and I can't begin to express my gratitude to these kind friends of my aunt Ella, my dear friends, and wonderful rabbis. The conversations and the reminiscing about Aunty did a world of good for me, and showed love and respect for Aunty, too.

OVERVIEW OF CHRONOLOGICAL EVENTS

Ella and Isadore were in hiding from February 1942 through the second day of Passover, April 1944. There was a ghetto established in Nagyszöllös, Hungary where they were already hiding. From April 1944 through early June 1944 they remained in this ghetto. They were then transported by cattle car to Auschwitz, Poland. Ella and her sister Olga were prisoners there until October 1944 when they were transferred to a labor camp in Nuremberg, Germany.

Isadore was transferred to Dachau labor camp in Germany.

Ella and Olga were then transferred to a labor camp in Holýšov, Czechoslovakia in February 1945.

Liberation of Dachau labor camp by Americans: April 29, 1945

Liberation of Holýšov labor camp by Americans: May 7, 1945

Ella reunited with Isadore: Summer (July/August) 1945

AUTHOR'S NOTE

The following map represents todays (2014) map of Eastern Europe. All the cities and towns remain in the same location as was seventy years ago. However, during the war years and for a number of years that followed, the borders changed several times. Therefore the shape of the map also has changed.

The cities and towns which are written on the map show the locations that Ella and Isadore Reich as well as Ella and her sister Olga Strauss (Gottesman) were in between the years of 1942-1945.

The Czech Republic and Slovakia were together during the war years and was known as Czechoslovakia.

All city borders are approximate.

In February 1942, Ella and Isadore Reich went into hiding. The following key to the map on the opposite page documents the cities and countries to which they fled, the location of concentration camps they were each imprisoned and their journey to get back home after the war in 1945:

1. Sečovce, Slovakia

2. Oborin, Slovakia

3. Király-Helmec, Hungary (Hungarian name) same as Kralovsky Chlmec (today Slovakia)

4. Miskolc, Hungary

5. Budapest, Hungary

6. Király-Helmec, Hungary

7. Iloncza, Hungary

8. Nagyszöllös, Hungary

9. Auschwitz (Oswiecim), Poland- Ella and Isadore imprisoned as well as Olga Strauss, Ella's sister

10. Nuremberg, Germany- Olga and Ella imprisoned in labor camp

11. Dachau, Germany- Isadore imprisoned in labor camp

12. Holýšov, Czechoslovakia- Olga and Ella imprisoned in labor camp

13. Prague, Czechoslovakia

14. Brno, Czechoslovakia

15. Morava, Czechoslovakia

16. Bratislava, Slovakia

17. Budapest, Hungary

18. Košice, Slovakia

19. Sečovce, Slovakia

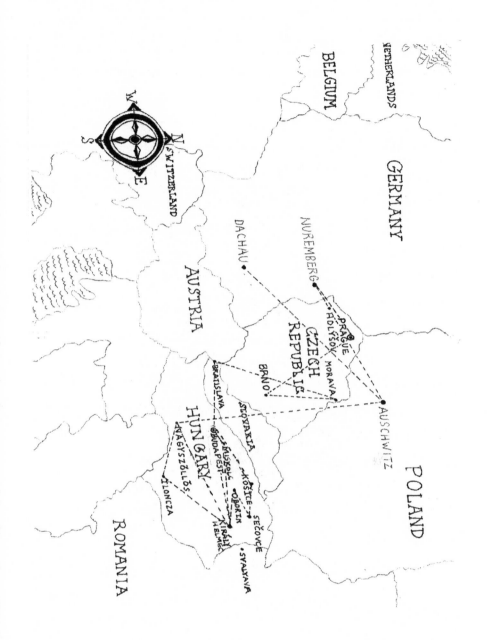

Ernő Hecht, Hungarian
Army, 1943

VOICES FROM THE PAST

In 1939, my mother's younger brother, Ernő, was drafted into the Hungarian army. The family kept numerous pictures and postcards of correspondence between my grandfather, David Hecht, and his son. While I was going through my aunt's belongings, I came across these seventy-five year old treasures that I had never known about. It amazes me, the depth of how Aunty cherished these memories to hold onto them forever, and in turn, to hold onto her past and never let it go. I found a Hungarian speaker to translate into English these family exchanges, and it helped line up all the dots in the sequence of events that was simultaneously occurring between the years of 1939-1943. As I had them read to me, I was touched by the closeness and openness of expression between my twenty-one year old uncle, whom I unfortunately never knew, and his beloved family. While Aunty and Uncle were on the run and in hiding, between 1942-1944, these correspondences were taking place. Also during this time, my mother had gotten married in 1941 and her husband had been taken to a Russian prison camp one year later, at the end of 1942, where he had died.

On the following pages I have included seven postcards in sequential order:

(The stamp on front indicates that it has been censored after reading postcard)

To:

Hecht, David

Abara

Deregnyo, Ungarn (Hungary in German)

From:

Hecht, Ernő

35/3.7 (Labor battalion. Ernő was on a base assigned to this unit.)

18- base post number

January 29, 1940

My dear parents and siblings,

I got the card yesterday, but I was waiting for a long letter. The weather here changes. Sometimes it's windy, but so far we can tolerate it. Last week it snowed a lot. We have a lot of work with it. Last week, again we went to target practice. There were three types. In two of them I was a marksman and in one a sharp shooter. We had maneuvers, but it was impeded by the snow. I did not participate because I was on sick call. Otherwise, I am well. Nothing hurts me. I have everything I need. Typically we only have maneuvers when the frost melts. I'm afraid that once more we're going to be recruits. There are more people coming here from Koszagi and Bornyekerol. I'm running out of time. What is the news at home? How are you? How is Olga feeling? Zoli--I wish you a Happy Birthday with lots of love. Olga, Fellner sends his regards and lots of kisses.

Hecht, Ernő Infantry

Koszeg--Unit 7th Battalion

Please write often about everything

[Same location as previous card]

July 28, 1940

My dear parents and siblings,

I received on the 23rd or 24th something that I've been waiting for patiently to get. Unfortunately, I couldn't go, however it's possible that in 2-3 weeks they might let me go home [It will be his turn]. How is Blanki [Blanka, his younger sister]?

Is there any hope that they will give us back the business? Is it possible to imagine my feelings. However, I believe that G-d will make everything good. If you're going to write, write a card and also more frequently because it's cheaper. Everyday it's raining so there is mud everywhere. . . . What is Izidor up to and how are they [Aunt Ella and her husband?]

I send many kisses to everybody,

Ernő

The information I learned through this correspondence was that my uncle's hope of returning home was false. Once enlisted in the army, there was no chance of being dismissed. I also learned that as early as 1940 in Hungary, my family's business--the general store they ran from their home--was confiscated. It was part of the pattern of events for Jews around Europe: they were branded, their businesses were stripped from them, their property was seized, and eventually they themselves were carted away to concentration camps.

[Same location as previous cards]

August 11, 1940

My dear parents and siblings,

I got the card that was written on the 7th. My dear mother, you write that I write too infrequently, but every week I write on two occasions. The leave that I was anticipating is going to be cancelled. I believe it will only happen if we are dismissed permanently. In the near term we are going to have an assignment.

I am very happy that Ella and Rozsika are well. Thank G-d I am also. The weather is starting to heat up. I am writing this card in the synagogue. When we have time we always go. The time is going nicely.

Blanki--does she know how to sew?

I kiss everybody very many times.

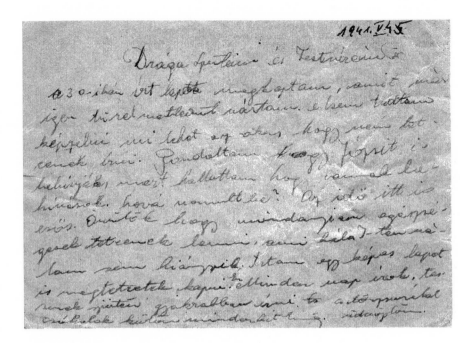

May 4, 1941

My dear parents and siblings,

The anticipated letter that I was waiting for arrived on the 30th [April]. I thought that I knew what the reason was that you didn't write. I thought that Jozsef [my mother Olga's first husband] got called up because I heard that there are further call-ups. To where was he drafted? The weather here is rainy....I'm writing everyday and I'd like my siblings to write more frequently.

I send all my love and kisses to everybody.

New unit he was transferred to:

Unit ID--103/ 5 (battalion)

40/ 52 (Base #)

May 5, 1939 (Ernő – second from left with X over his head)

Until late 1939, there were Jews in the military who were clothed and armed just like any other soldier. In Hungary, the government enacted laws applicable to Jews restricting movement, occupation, ownership of land, and who Jews could marry. For example, a Jew couldn't marry a gentile by law. Around mid-1940, they passed more restrictive laws on the Jews:

1. Jews could not bear arms in the military. Weapons were confiscated from those Jews who had them.
2. Jews had to wear yellow armbands or white armbands. If you had one Jewish grandparent, you wore white. These soldiers professed not to be Jewish, but the laws that were passed proclaimed if you had at least one Jewish grandparent, you were Jewish.

January 1941, Király Mezo

Soldiers are wearing heavy coats meaning conditions were still good. These people in picture were clearly Hungarian units who were defined by their hats. Until after the Germans attacked the Soviets, the labor battalions were treated humanely, meaning they were given food rations.

(Written on a civilian postcard with no military censor involved)

May 25, 1941

My dear parents and siblings,

I don't even know how to begin writing this letter. A lot of things are happening, but I can't write about it all. I'm only writing this if by some chance you haven't mailed the package yet.

Please don't send the bathing suit because it would be confiscated. If by chance you receive these cards infrequently, don't be alarmed because there are limits on these. Thank G-d I am well. There is not that much to write. We read that there was a lot of water at the base of the Carpathian Mountains. We also had rains in this area. . . I can't write anymore. I send my kisses and regards to everybody.

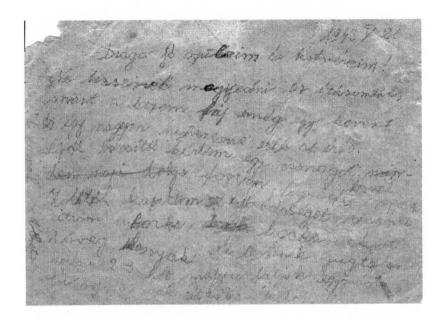

[Letter not censored and not on base]

May 26, 1943

My dear parents and siblings,

Please don't be frightened about my writing because my hand still hurts. The writing is very difficult for me. I asked for a package from Lajos. I got from Zoltan [younger brother] two packages: orange, lemon, pickles, sugar cubes, one bottle of cognac.

Please don't be uneasy because in 2-3 weeks we're going to be able to see each other. . . . If you're going to send another package, please make sure that you include sweets and if possible [some kind of] noodle with which I can make something. I thank you for the chocolate that you sent.

Hecht, Ernő

Munkacs

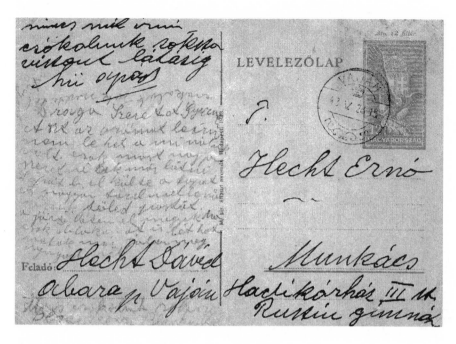

(letter from David Hecht to his son, Ernő)

May 28, 1943

My dear son,

I write to you in happiness when I found out that you're going to be in Munkacs, so on Monday I tried to go to you, but unfortunately I couldn't see you. But we hope that the time will come that we see each other with G-d's help. Thank G-d that He made it possible for you to be here. G-d will continue to help you. I told Zlovkanak that he should give you everything that you would ask for. Therefore, whatever you have a need for and is allowed to be sent in, just write and ask for it and we're going to send it. Until now we haven't received from you any request. At home everything is fine. Here there's nothing unusual to write. We kiss you a lot of times until we meet again. With warm regards.

(Note from Margit Hecht, Ernő's mother, my grandmother)

My dear loving son,

I can't write how much I miss you over time passed. I would like to see you very much. At this time I would laugh a lot and be happy if I could see your face. We're waiting to get a letter from you. . . . You should stay calm. Ella also sends many kisses, (as well as) Olga, Rozsi, Blanki, Zoli.

David Hecht

Abara, Vajoiu (Hungary)

In all, there were eleven postcards between Ernő and his family. I learned from their exchange that even when family is separated and circumstances are difficult, their faith and belief in G-d stayed strong. Their loving words also kept them strong.

Who knows if I'll ever visit the cities that my parents grew up in all those years ago, but at least I and my children can get a small taste of how things looked back then, as well as savoring the beautiful pictures and incredible stories about my family and their origins. I feel very blessed to have come from such a background.

OUR CHILDREN'S WEDDING, A NEW BEGINNING

(L to R) Dovid, Yaakov, Azi, Rivki, Miriam and Asher

Almost six weeks after Aunty had passed away, my beautiful daughter's wedding was to take place. Naturally, Aunty was on my mind, but I needed to focus on wedding preparations, and helping Rivki set up her and her husband's new home. Can you guess where their new lives would begin?

As human beings, we can't understand the plans or timing of events. I believe people often blame G-d, but don't see the "hand" of G-d in the bigger scheme of things, only in the day- to-day occurrences.

Rivki and Azi had summer jobs planned, but they wouldn't start until two weeks after they got married, and didn't know where they could go during the interim. Little did any of us know how things would work out. Aunty literally gave the kids her apartment as a wedding gift from heaven above! Now the excitement would begin. I had finished teaching for the school year, and Rivki had graduated from college (summa cum laude). Now, our full attention was on shopping and cleaning the young couple's apartment. I wouldn't trade that special time with my daughter for anything. An added blessing was that the children had a fully furnished home! They inherited a lovely bedroom set, dining room table and chairs, sofa, recliner, and end tables. I was also able finally to get rid of a storage rental by giving them my father's breakfront and headboard. Thank G-d, they had everything they needed and more!

The big day came, and the *chatan*, bridegroom and *kallah*, bride, looked radiant. It was a beautiful wedding. I woke up the next morning feeling sad. Yaakov left for work as usual, Asher went to his summer job, Dovid went to class, and I was alone. I started crying. There were no more wedding plans to busy myself with, Rivki wasn't home, and Aunty was gone. I sat on my daughter's bed and just cried. I felt as if I had no one to take care of. I spoke with a social worker who is a friend of mine, and described how I felt. She said the most amazing thing. "Miriam, this is a loss, and it's normal to feel this way." This made perfect sense and explained my behavior. Since then, when other mothers in a similar situation hear how I felt, they admit that they cried, too. The joy I felt on Rivki's wedding day wasn't diminished. This was a new adjustment period in my life. My parents, aunt, and uncle were gone, my children were all grown, and my daughter was starting her new life. It was a lot to take in at once.

Luckily, we had *sheva brachot*, seven days of celebration, and that kept my mind occupied. I was also happily surprised that Rivki and Azi were stopping by daily to visit. It was wonderful to see how well Asher, Dovid, and Azi got along. Rivki came by to play the piano, Azi would play the guitar with his father-in-law, and Dovid would accompany them on the drums. Azi would invite me to play some music games with him, Dovid, and Asher. Plus, we had numerous dinners and *Shabbos* meals together as a family--now the six of us! I told Azi that I could get used to this, and he smiled. It's nice to know that your son-in-law likes to spend time with his in-laws. The truth is, he fits in beautifully with our family, thank G-d. We are very fortunate.

The kids enjoyed the apartment very much over the next couple of weeks, and for another three weeks after their return. The question now was whether they should continue to live here and commute, or move closer to Rivki's graduate school? The latter won out. It really was for the best. Even though Aunty's home was a free apartment, the commute would have taken Rivki almost two hours, and driving home some nights would also have been very difficult. They were so grateful to have had Aunty's apartment to begin their married life together. Now, the question was: What to do with it? As with everything, G-d had plans. There is a Jewish expression, "Three times is a *chazaka* [strength]." It seems that this apartment was to be rented by another newly married couple for a year-and-a-half, furnished with my parents bedroom set, and recently yet another young married couple began renting it. They invited us to their wedding and the lovely bride said to me, "The apartment really looks like a home." They decorated the place lovingly. It made me happy that I could loan them my parents bedroom set, and especially that Aunty's home could be a home for young couples to start their new lives together.

Rivki married an unusual boy. It's wonderful to watch the two of them together--how they laugh and get along, thank G-d, so beautifully. The unusual part is how comfortable and open he is with Yaakov and me. Numerous times in the two-plus years since they married, different circumstances have arisen in which he has shown us how truly appreciative he is of his wife's parents. For example, less than half a year after they got married, we were discussing the real possibility of a job opening in our *shul* as youth director. He sent me an email: "I realize that I don't thank you nearly enough for all the support (not just financial) you have been giving us to make our first year together as wonderful as it is, and I am very proud to consider you guys my parents. With love, Azi."

Two short years later, when Azi graduated from his studies in social work, he looked me in the eye and said, "I couldn't have done these two years without you." Azi has a great relationship with Yaakov. They play music together and share similar interests. As for me, he compliments me often and lets me know that he likes my cooking, especially soups. He also thinks I have good taste in clothing. He especially likes the *Shabbos* coat he received on *Chanukah*, the winter coat he got as a birthday present, and all the shirts he received for *afikoman* (a piece of matzah hidden then found, for which the finder receives a reward on Passover). He knows full well that he is part of our family and is looked upon as a son. It's for this reason that I can talk to him about important matters. He asks my opinion and he is respectful and takes my advice and suggestions to heart because he knows it's meant for his (and their) benefit.

Time passed and new events began to shape our lives. Asher was in his first year of college and chose psychology as his major. Dovid finished a degree in broadcasting and was in the middle of an internship at a radio station while looking for full-time employment. Azi was in his last year of graduate school, and Rivki was in her second year of graduate school and teaching music in a local *yeshiva*. We would get together with Rivki and Azi sometimes once a week, other times, every two weeks. We've been invited to their apartment several times for *Shabbos*, and had a wonderful time being with them and meeting their friends and rabbi. Rivki and I would talk daily, and something about her seemed different, but in a good way. A mother knows her children, and when you and your daughter have a bond and close relationship, you know her moods and personality. Rivki came for a visit one Sunday and she looked different somehow. I asked her, "Are you pregnant?" and she said, "Yes!"

We hugged each other fiercely, and we both cried happy tears. They had been married almost seventeen months. It was also still *very* early on. We saw each other at a wedding one week later, and with a big smile I wished Azi, *"b'sha'ah tova,"* it should be in good time. He said, quite happily, "We wanted to wait to tell people, but I'm really happy Rivki told you, because she needs her mother to talk to." That meant a lot to me.

In Judaism, it is customary to name a child after a loved one who is deceased. It is a way of giving honor and paying tribute to his or her memory. A name shows permanence. A name means everything.

When I was pregnant with my first child, Aunty approached me during my second trimester and said very seriously, "If it's a boy, I would like you to name him after my father, Dovid," and I replied, "I don't think that should be a problem, but I will discuss it with Yaakov." Yaakov was fine with that name. When Rivki was four months along, I too sat down with her and told her, "If the baby is a boy, I would like him named after my father, your *zaidy* and if it's a girl, for her to be named after Aunty Ella, who was like a mother to me." Rivki said, "Mommy, I know what you want, I want it also. This is emotional for me, too. Azi and I will discuss it." I knew Rivki would want her *zaidy*'s name passed on to her child if it were a boy; she loved him dearly. I've heard her telling Azi what a cute, sweet man he was. And if it were a girl, she would want to name her after Aunty because she loved her deeply and had a close relationship with her.

This was the first time that Yaakov and I were becoming grandparents, and it was very emotional for us both. Thank G-d, Yaakov's parents were about to become great-grandparents. What a blessing. Yaakov understood completely how I felt, but reminded me that choosing a name was the children's decision. I understood and agreed, so for the next five months I kept quiet and hoped.

As the time to give birth approached, Rivki and I discussed carriages, cribs, and car seats--among other things—and, of course, our plans to babysit two evenings a week while she continued going to graduate school for music therapy. Our son-in-law had graduated with a Master of Social Work (MSW) degree and has been diligently searching for work.

Rivki had invited me numerous times to come with her to the obstetrician. Nowadays, sonograms are taken frequently and precautions, more seriously. The first time I saw the baby on the screen, I gasped and started to cry. Rivki took my hand and held it tight. What a sight to see the fingers, heart, and head. The technician asked Rivki if she wanted to know the gender of the baby, but she said no.

Rivki's due date was fast approaching, but little in the way of preparations took place. It may seem superstitious, but there was no shopping for anything. Nor was there a baby shower. We believe it's better not to invite the evil eye. However, we did discuss necessities for the baby, and the like. My in-laws offered to buy a car seat and a stroller. Yaakov and I still had the crib from when our children were babies and we would borrow a bassinet, and buy a Pack 'n' Play and other accessories.

Excitement and anticipation filled the air as we waited for our new arrival to make his or her way into the world.

REFLECTING ON THE PAST IS OUR HOPE FOR THE FUTURE

We experience many kinds of love in life, but there is no greater love and bond than that between a parent and a child. During a child's growth and upbringing, you put your heart and soul into raising him to be a mensch--a good, upstanding human being. Children truly see every good--and not-so-good--deed we do as parents. When they get older, they have decisions to make: Do I follow my parents' example for the good they displayed in their lives? Or do I observe the negative aspects of their behavior, and fall into that way of life? We are our children's role models and guides throughout their lives, not just while they are living under our roof. Parenting is an awesome responsibility.

When a parent passes away, the period of mourning is different than that for the other five close relatives. For a sister, brother, husband, wife, and child, the mourning ends with *Shloshim* (first thirty days of mourning). For parents, we mourn a full year. We attend no weddings, concerts, parties or celebration of any kind, except to get married or to attend our own child's wedding. This is Hashem's way of telling us, there is no stronger bond than the one between parent and child, and a child should have that much respect for a parent, even after his or her passing. My memories of my four parents are very clear. I learned much from each of them about how to conduct my life.

Miriam with Aunt Ella and Uncle Isadore Reich

Miriam with Parents, Morris and Olga Gottesman

I was speaking recently with Nomi's daughter, Roni, who lives in Israel with her family. I described the book I was writing and she said, "Miriam, you weren't supposed to be here. You are a walking miracle." We will never understand why some lives were cut short by this horrific tragedy of the Holocaust, while others survived and went on to rebuild their lives and have beautiful families. All I know is that the older (and wiser) I become, thank G-d,

I feel indebted to my four parents for all they did for me during their lives. I was very lucky, indeed, to have had my aunt and uncle to pick up where my mother and father had to leave off. Now Yaakov and I have raised three wonderful children and even though they are adults, we are still, thank G-d, able to be there for them when they need our help and advice.

Do I know the full reason why Hashem allowed these four amazing individuals to survive? I believe that for the most part I do: To bring new life into this world, and to raise this life in the traditions and faith in which that they were raised. In response to this, this child grew up, and in Aunty's own words:

"My sister got married in '53. After eleven years of marriage, she gave birth to a little girl. We never had children. What a happy occasion. This little girl, Miriam Gottesman, grew up. She finished college. She's a teacher. She got married. Very nice Jewish family. And now she is a happy mother with three kids, living a beautiful Jewish life."

MAZAL TOV! IT'S A GIRL

Mazal tov! Rivki and Azi are the proud parents of a beautiful baby girl. She weighs seven pounds, three ounces, and is nineteen inches long. She has a full head of dark hair with blond highlights, and sparkling blue eyes. She was born in the summer of 2013. We love her already.

For a boy, we wait until the eighth day of life to have a *bris*, but for a girl we name her on the first Monday, Thursday, or *Shabbos* after her birth, when we read from the Torah. Azi and Rivki were ready the next morning (Thursday) to give their daughter a name. The previous evening, unbeknownst to my family (except for Yaakov) I felt a strong need to go visit the graves of my beloved parents, aunt and uncle. I recited some *tehillim*, talked to them, then returned to visit Rivki and the baby.

Yaakov, Dovid, Asher and Azi left that morning to go to shul where the naming would take place. I too, got up early--not to go with them, but to go visit Rivki at the hospital. She asked me if Daddy or Azi had called me to inform me of the name. I told her I didn't want to hear it from them, but from her. She said, "*Esther.*"

We hugged and kissed each other, and I thanked her because Aunty now has a namesake. Mostly, I thanked G-d. If this precious little girl can grow up to possess the qualities similar to that of her namesake - a woman of strength, determination, intelligence, kindness, empathy, integrity, and love-she will go very far in life. My daughter, Rivka, is named for my mother, and now my granddaughter, Esther, is named for her sister. The circle is complete.

What a perfect ending to my story, or shall I say, what a perfect beginning to a new life.

Miriam with Daughter Rivki and Granddaughter Esther

EPILOGUE

We entered the camp walking on the train tracks; the same tracks that had carried the cattle cars that brought my family there. Walking down a long path, we didn't know what we would find. As we continued along the path we had no choice but to turn left.

In front of our eyes we saw the gas chambers and crematorium in ruins. There, people had been told to remove their clothes, strangers looking at each other. Fathers seeing their children, children seeing their fathers. No more dignity, no more privacy.

From there we walked to where the women's barracks had stood. **Lager C** was for the Hungarian women. "Barrack 31, right Miriam?" The tour guide asked me for verification. "Yes, that's what my aunt told me. She and my mother were there with their family." There were columns in front of each and every barrack with its number printed on it. The large open area where the barracks had been went further than the eye could see. The concrete foundation encased a large rectangle where the barracks had once stood. The bunk beds on the right and left sides of the room were no longer there, but the remnants of the chimney down the middle remained, just as Aunty had described it. Afterwards, Yaakov and I walked together to Barrack 28, where Mommy and Aunty were moved after a selection.

We rejoined our group, which were already a distance away, waiting for the next segment in the sequence of events.

Tzvi, our guide explained, "The problem for the Nazis wasn't killing the Jews, the problem was what to do with all the bodies." After the bodies were burned in the crematorium the Nazis had to dispose of the ashes. We looked down to see two massive pits filled with green water, like a pond. There were too many frogs to count jumping in and out of the water. Tzvi explained that when ashes (from body fat) are mixed with water, concrete forms. Over time these "ponds" formed because the water had no place to seep through.

My mind couldn't comprehend what I was seeing before my eyes. These ashes were my grandparents, aunts, and uncles. It was impossible to grasp such a concept that my family was murdered and buried as ash within these pits, together with millions of others. In my hands I held a small photo album which I put together before our trip. It contained old family pictures that I found amongst Aunty's possessions. I looked intently at the Hecht family photo from 1935, taken shortly after Aunty and Uncle were married. I knew I wanted to speak, but never imagined it would be in this spot. I looked upon this and the words just flowed out of my mouth.

"This isn't you. You may have died here physically, but you aren't dead. I am speaking to my grandparents, aunts, and uncles on my mother's side and on my father's side. You live through me. You live on through your surviving daughters, Olga and Ella. You have a great-granddaughter, my daughter, Rivka named after your daughter, Olga. And I have a granddaughter, your great- great granddaughter, Esther, named after your daughter, Ella. So you did not die here. I love you from all the stories I've been told about you and so you will continue to live on."

This was the eulogy my family never had. [YouTube video entitled: "You Live Through Me - Auschwitz." Follow link from www.Iambecauseofyou.net]

As we walked past the barbed wire surrounding us, I heard an audible sound like something tearing. I looked down at my skirt and the hem was torn. It had gotten caught on the barbed wire. I showed this to some friends and they said, "You just did *kriah.*"

After the trip to Poland, we all returned to the airport. Our first leg of the trip was over, and while our group went back to New York, Yaakov and I continued on with our journey. This was a trip of a lifetime and while we were already in Eastern Europe, we had made plans to continue on to the towns from which my parents originated.

We made our plans months in advance and hired a Jewish tour guide, Bela (we called him by his Hebrew name, Baruch), who lives in West Ukraine. He speaks Hungarian, Russian, English, Yiddish, and Hebrew. He was wonderful, helpful, and knowledgeable, all of which was indispensable.

I will go out of sequence for the next piece of our journey.

We crossed the border from Slovakia into Ukraine and stayed in Munkachevo (Munkacs) for the night. The next morning we went to my father's town of Svalyava. We made arrangements ahead of time to meet with a friend of a friend who lives there. This gentleman did some research by talking to people and found an older gentleman who said he remembered the Gottesman family and that they lived on Partisanska Street, so we crossed a bridge over the Tatoriza River, then crossed another bridge over a creek.

We then entered the Bistriy district. This was the beginning of Partisanska Street, which had been the Jewish area over seventy years ago. While driving down this street, our new friend said, "This can't be right, it's too far down on Partisanska. The Jews lived closer to the center of town because that's where the synagogues were." There were no more of the old houses, he explained because when the Communists came in they knocked all the old houses down and built new.

"How many people live in Svalyava now?" I asked.

"Eighteen thousand." He replied.

"And back in the early 1940s?" I enquired.

"Ten thousand, almost half were Jewish." He answered.

He said there are no more Jews in Svalyava today.

"What a loss for our people," I thought.

We then went to the Svalyava Jewish cemetery in the hope of finding the graves of my father's four young siblings who all died under the age of twelve due to disease. We asked the cemetery keeper where children would be buried and he pointed along the side wall. Jewish people believe it is very tragic when a child dies so we place their graves off to the side to make their graves less noticeable.

Yaakov and I looked over every tombstone in the cemetery. Numerous stones had eroded over time, some hardly legible. Some were leaning over and too heavy to lift, and some had heavy brush growing over them that couldn't be pulled away. Yaakov tried, but the stones were too heavy and the brush to deep. Unfortunately, we couldn't find even one tombstone belonging to my family. We were told that when the Germans came into these towns and cities, they would desecrate the cemeteries by throwing the tombstones around and breaking them. I told Yaakov, "For all we know, we could be walking on top of their graves." Yaakov said a *Kel Maaleh*, a special prayer for the dead and included all four of the children's Hebrew names. I asked the cemetery keeper how old this cemetery was and he said, "Three hundred and seventy-four years old."

We washed our hands as is customary to do when leaving a cemetery and the cemetery keeper kindly volunteered to take us to the house of the former mayor of Svalyava. We had made arrangements to meet with him ahead of time.

We met in his backyard and the first thing he did was take my hand and kiss it. Very old world and sweet. I giggled. This gesture reminded me of my father. When he would greet a woman, he would always bow his head and tip his hat.

The mayor was referred to as "Mishko," but I called him "Mr. Mishko." He was eighty-five years old and had served as mayor for thirty years. He said that he remembered the Gottesman family.

"The Gottesman family was famous."

I asked what they did for a living.

He said, "They owned a grocery store."

"Was it in front of their house?" I asked.

"Next to their house." He responded.

"What did they sell?" I wanted to know.

"Everything. They owned a chain of stores. They did business in other cities." He replied.

I was testing his memory, and he was correct, from what my father told me. The family grocery store was where my father learned to do business.

Mr. Mishko explained further. "The Jews lived on Szido Utca [Jeedoe Utza= Jew Street]." This wasn't a derogatory term, just a fact.

"This was the center of town. All the Jews lived there and had their businesses there because they had to be close to their synagogues, which were there."

He continued, "The rich Jews had their own synagogue and the poor Jews had their synagogue. This area was known as the Main Road. Main Road was all Jewish except for four families." This was all true. My father told me that the majority was Jewish with a few non-Jews living there.

We thanked him for the information and drove to the center of town which is Partisanska Street today. There was no Gottesman house any longer, but it was good to see the area where my family lived.

Before we traveled to Svalyava, our first stop the day before was to Oborin, Slovakia, where my mother had lived. Before we left home, I had listened intently to Aunty's Shoah video because she left distinct landmarks indicating where the Hecht family house was located. With her hands she demonstratively explained, "Our house was the last house on the street. We lived on the bank of a lake and the church was that way [across from their house]."

When we arrived, our first stop was the municipality. Baruch spoke in Hungarian and asked for archival records. They said they weren't there. I had hoped we would be able to find out the house address of my grandparents from long ago. We then asked if there were any older people still here and they told us of a certain gentleman. Then we asked where the church was and they told us. We drove in that direction and Yaakov saw the church so we parked the car. Baruch asked a gentleman on a bicycle about this older man we were looking for, and he pointed in one direction. Then Baruch asked if there were any other older people and he pointed to a house across from the church.

He then asked, "Is she Jewish?"

"Yes," replied Baruch.

"She looks Jewish," he said. I had to laugh.

I told Baruch we should stay in this area because the church was here. Aunty told me where she grew up was a village of maybe a thousand people. It seems to be a similar population today.

As we walked a little closer, we saw the lake to the left of us. I started getting anxious.

There were three construction workers working on the side of the church and Baruch asked if there were any older people living here. One gentleman crossed the sidewalk, opened a gate, and knocked on a door. An older woman came out to greet us. Baruch asked in Hungarian, "Was there a family by the name Hecht who used to live here?"

She nodded yes and pointed to the house next door to hers! This was incredible and exactly as Aunty had described: "The last house on the street, on the bank of a lake," and the church was right across from their house. I began to cry. Then she started talking about the Hecht family. I asked Baruch to explain everything to me that she was saying.

I took out my photo album with several pictures from the 1930s and 1940s. I showed her the Hecht family photo from 1935 and in the blink of an eye she pointed to each person and said, "Dovid Bacsi, Margit Neni, Ernő, Olga, Ella, Rozsi, Blanka, Zoli."

When she said, "Olga," I screamed, "That's my mother."

I started crying again.

She remembered each family member though she was only ten years old in 1944. They were not just next-door neighbors, but clearly friends with the Hecht family. We spent at least an hour speaking with her. Everything I asked, she answered accurately according to what Aunty had told me.

"What is your name?" I asked.

"Aranka," she replied.

Aranka told me that Dovid Bacsi would invite her to sit on their porch and he would talk to her. Aranka described my grandfather as a "close friend."

The Hecht house was built of stone and painted white with a metal roof.

"What did my grandparents do for a living?" I asked.

"They had a store right in front of the house. There was a plum tree in front."

"What did they sell?"

"Everything." (It was like a supermarket.)

She said that she would light the fire for them on Shabbos. She remembered what a religious man my grandfather was. He would pray daily with something on his head and his hand (phylacteries). She pointed to the well on the Hecht property and said her family shared the well. She said my grandparents were very nice people, very good people, good neighbors.

Aranka said, "Zoli went to Ungvar [Hungarian name for city of Uzhhorod which today is in West Ukraine, on the border with Slovakia] to high school to learn the German language. He went with a neighbor and came home for Shabbos. There was a tree in front of the house where Zoli and his friend would sit and study German." She said Zoli was very smart and she would learn German from him. He would go by horse-drawn carriage or bicycle to the train station and went to Ungvar by train.

Baruch explained later that if the family could afford to send their son to attend an out-of-town school and come home for Shabbos, they were well-off. My mother rode a bicycle, and he said that in those days it was the equivalent of a car. It was a good feeling to know that my family had lacked for nothing and had been comfortable.

She remembered Ernő was a tall, handsome man.

She remembered my mother's wedding. I asked where it had taken place and she pointed to where a pole now stood. This was exactly where Aunty had said it was: in a big open space in front of the house and across from the church. Aranka demonstrated the poles that served as the chuppah with a covering on top and how the glass was broken by the foot of the groom, and how my grandmother wore a wig on her head.

I asked about the description of the inside of the house and she said, "The store was in the front, then there was a hall from the shop into the house. Then there were two small rooms, a pantry and kitchen, and a place for the cow out back." This was exactly as Aunty had described it.

She remembered the deportation. It was warm, summer because she was wearing light clothing. She pointed to the sidewalk and said, "When they [Hungarian police] started to collect them and sit them on the horse wagon, Dovid Bacsi asked my grandmother for two loaves of bread and said he would give it back when he returned." She said they were old people and they didn't say goodbye because they expected to come back. They took whatever they could. The deportation was a surprise; they had no idea the police were coming for them. They thought this was temporary.

I asked who else was taken. She said, "Erno, Zoli, Rozsi, Olga and Blanki. Ella wasn't there."

I asked, "Who came back after the war?"

"Ella and Olga," she answered.

"How did they look?" I wanted to know.

I knew a few months had passed between liberation for Ella and Olga and coming back to their parents' home. It was summertime. Ella had been reunited with her husband, Isadore, in Sečovce, where they had lived prior to going into hiding and the three of them needed to get their strength back.

"Not too thin, but very sad. Olga told me about the crematorium. We wrote to each other for a while [when Olga was in the United States she sent three letters to Aranka's grandmother]. When they came back, they slept here and just stayed for a week. Olga asked my mother for a knife. They [Olga and Ella] went into their own house and into the kitchen. Olga went to the oven and scraped between the bricks and they dug out from (behind the bricks) in front of the oven a little chest, but I don't know what was inside." *I had never heard this before. Aunty told me they had buried valuables before they were taken away, but I had no idea where. They knew the deportation would eventually come and so they buried things of value to have upon their return. Tragically, almost no families returned.*

I asked what had happened to the house. Aranka explained, "The Germans came first, then the Hungarians. The house was totally empty. The soldiers used the Hecht house to put their horses in and also they used the church for the same purpose. Then on November 17, 1944, the Russians came and used the furniture from the house for firewood and also as a place to store their weapons.

They slept in the church." Baruch explained that this wasn't uncommon. The Russians came to this part of the country around November 1944.

Aranka said she had some photos. She went to look and came back with only one photo she could find. It was of my Aunt Rozsika and Aunt Blanka. She asked if I would like to have it and I thanked her and added it to my album.

She was very nice and kind to us. Many neighbors would have rejected our visit. It appears that our families were good neighbors and friendly toward each other.

Aranka answered my many questions. Finally, I couldn't think of anything further to ask. I said to Baruch, "I want to give her something. How much should I give her?"

"Give her twenty dollars," he suggested.

I took Aranka's hand and folded the bill into it while holding her hand.

"What for? I don't need it," she said.

I started to cry again and said, "You don't know what you have done for me."

This complete stranger who was a neighbor and childhood friend to my family had brought closure for me. I wanted to show appreciation. I hugged her and thanked her.

Later in the car I said to Yaakov and to Baruch, "I paid back the bread for my grandfather."

Now my dear grandfather, you owe nothing and you can rest in peace.

[YouTube video entitled: Miraculous Meeting. Follow link from www.Iambecauseofyou.net]

The Hecht Family, 1935

Back row (l to r): Blanka, Ernő, Olga, Ella (Hecht) and Isadore Reich, Rozsika

Front row (l to r): David, Zolika, Margit

Miriam Dobin in front of the Hecht family home, Oborin, Slovakia, 2014.

AUDIO AND VIDEO

Please visit my website at www.Iambecauseofyou.net.

There you will find links to:

- An audio recording of Ella's story as *she* describes her experiences from 1942-1945.

- The YouTube video, "You Live Through Me - Auschwitz" – My visit to Auschwitz concentration camp in 2014.

- The YouTube video, "Miraculous Meeting" – My unexpected meeting with the Hecht family's neighbor.

A link to the website can also be found on my Facebook page – "I Am Because Of You."

ACKNOWLEDGEMENTS

For a number of years, I've known that I wanted to write this book about my family. When my father was still here, our lives were so involved with his care that it was impossible to write. Then caring for my aunt overlapped with the passing of my father. Shortly after Aunty died, my daughter got married. At that time, I made a commitment to myself that I would sit down over my next summer vacation and begin writing, and so I did. This history of the Hecht--Gottesman--Reich families is my gift to my children and especially, to my beautiful granddaughter, Esther, to pass down to all future generations as a living legacy to the amazing family from which she has come.

First and foremost, I want to thank *Hashem* for having given me the strength and determination to follow through. This challenge took twenty- two months to complete, but I did it with His help.

Next, my thanks to the lovely Hanina Hanoch for spending numerous hours translating my father's documents from German into English for me, and for meeting with my father back in 2000, three years before his passing, to translate his story into German for the purpose of seeking reparations. Hanina, you are a gem.

To Joshua Braunstein: After reading the manuscript cover to cover, you took even more time out of your busy schedule to collaborate with me to choose a title that captures the true essence of the book. Thank you for all your kindness.

To Michelle Russo - McLaughlin: Thank you for working with me on the cover design of this book. The saying, "A picture is worth a thousand words" is so true. Your time and effort is truly appreciated.

To Martin Rajec, originally from Slovakia: Thank you for taking the time out of your busy schedule to translate the numerous documents from Slovak into English. Your kindness is truly appreciated.

To my friend and Hungarian translator, Gabor Boda: Thank you, thank you for translating the precious family postcards from over seventy years ago, as well as the video from our trip to Slovakia. Your knowledge and expertise on this portion of history was invaluable and helped put the chronology of events in its proper perspective. You and your lovely wife, Cindy have kind hearts and tremendous patience. Your time and effort on my family's history are forever appreciated.

To Sandra Webb: Thank you for copyediting my manuscript. I appreciate your interest in the subject matter. We share a deep commitment for our respective faiths and a strong belief in G-d.

To our Hungarian tour guide par excellence Bela Huber, or as we called you by your Hebrew name, Baruch: We couldn't have managed the trip to Slovakia and West Ukraine without your language skills, social skills, and knowledge of this area of Eastern Europe. I owe you much appreciation and gratitude for locating and emailing me copies of family birth and death records that are over one hundred years old. Thank you for your kindness, patience, sense of humor, persistence, and interest in my family's history.

To Mindy Waizer: Thank you for spending the time and making the effort to work with me on this project. It amazes me that as wives, mothers and career women we still can find the time to help others. To quote you as I left your home, "I really hope this works out for you." It did; thanks for your kindness.

To Azi Steiner: "My son-in-law the cartographer." Thank you for your professional drawing of the map of Eastern Europe. Your time and patience when reviewing Aunty and Uncle's difficult journey and researching historical maps relating to our family's history are very much appreciated. We can't wait to see what Esther will draw.

To Mela Cohen: Thank you for your professional drawing of the Perth Amboy street map as well as completing the map of my family's journey through Eastern Europe. Your help, artistic talent and efforts are very much appreciated.

To Tom Goldstein: Thank you very much for taking so much time out of your busy schedule to be the Hungarian to English translator and vice-versa between Aranka and me on several conference calls that were made recently. Being able to speak with her through you allowed us to fill in the gaps for the many questions I had after having miraculously met her in July of 2014. Your kindnesses are greatly appreciated.

To Rabbi Eliezer Kaminetzky, Rabbi Emeritus Congregation Ohav Emeth: Thank you for taking the time to translate my great-grandfather's will. Your efforts and kind words over the years are truly appreciated.

To Rabbi Eliyahu Kaufman, Rabbi, Congregation Ohav Emeth: Thank you for being a dear friend to my family and supporting us with your knowledge and kind words during a most difficult period in our lives.

To Beth Nilla: Thank you for helping me set up a Facebook page for my book. Your friendship and confidence over the years is heart-warming. I'm proud to have been a part of your daughters' lives.

To Dr. Jamie Wasserman: Thank you for reviewing my manuscript. Your opinion is truly appreciated. Your friendship and trust over the years has meant so much to me and always will. It has been a pleasure to have been a part of your daughters' lives.

To Dr. Jay Rovner, Manuscript Bibliographer for the Library of the Jewish Theological Seminary: Much thanks for explaining the will of my great-grandfather, Aleksander Hecht (1848-1934). You delved into the translation of some complicated phrases and helped simplify its content for my family to understand what a truly religious man he was. Your efforts are greatly appreciated.

To Rahel (Rosie) Baruh: Thank you my dear editor for all your time, effort and suggestions to make this book the best that it could be. You helped me look deeper within which allowed me to bring more of myself out. Who could have guessed that the long-standing friendship which our daughters continue to share would have been the catalyst that formed a bond between us. Now you and I share our own dear friendship based on honesty, trust, respect for one another's impressions and of course, banana bread and coffee ice cream.

Acharon acharon chaviv, save the best for last. To my family: Yaakov, your support of my efforts, coupled with tremendous patience, shows your love and respect for me, for this book, and for my convictions. Thank you for scanning in all the photos and documents, the countless hours sitting with me reviewing the manuscript, creating the website for this book and teaching me some necessary computer skills. I knew I married a good guy.

To my children, Dovid, Asher, Rivki, and Azi: Our beautiful family legacy is yours to pass along to future generations, please G-d. Thank you for your continuous love, support, advice, and encouragement: "You can do it, Mommy."

To my granddaughter, Esther: You are named after an amazing woman, my little love. Wear her name with pride, and G-d willing, when you are older, we'll go for walks and have long talks about your lovely great, great Aunty Ella.

GLOSSARY

Acharon acharon chaviv - (Hebrew) Whoever is most dear goes last.

Afikoman - (Hebrew) A piece of matzah broken in half from the middle one of the three matzot set before the leader of a Passover Seder: it is hidden by the leader and later searched for by the children, with the finder, usually the youngest, receiving a reward.

Appel - (German) A selection.

Ba'al Chesed - (Hebrew) One who performs acts of kindness and generosity.

Ba'al Shem Tov - (Hebrew) Founder of Chassidic movement in the 1700s. The title literally means "Master of the Good Name."

Baruch Hashem - (Hebrew) Blessed is G-d.

Bat Mitzvah - (Hebrew) Age of maturity for a girl (twelve years).

Bacsi – (Hungarian) Uncle.

Beis Medrash - (Hebrew) Study house or study hall.

Bekesha - (Yiddish) A black robe made of silk material usually worn on Shabbos.

Bikur Cholim - (Hebrew) Visiting the sick.

Bris/Brit Milah - (Hebrew) The ceremonial circumcision performed on a Jewish boy eight days after birth.

Brucha/Bracha - (Hebrew) a blessing.

B'shah'ah tova – (Hebrew) It should be at a good time.

Bubby - (Yiddish) grandmother.

Challah – (Hebrew) Special braided bread for *Shabbos*.

Chanukah - (Hebrew) Holiday celebrated for eight days beginning on the twenty-fifth day in the Hebrew month of Kislev (usually December).

Chassid - (Yiddish) One who is a member of a Jewish mystic movement founded in the eighteenth century in Eastern Europe by the Ba'al Shem Tov that reacted against Talmudic learning and maintained that G-d's presence was in all of one's surroundings and that one should serve G-d in one's every deed and word.

Chatan - (Hebrew) Bridegroom.

Chazaka - (Hebrew) Strength.

Cheder - (Yiddish) Elementary Jewish private school in which children are taught to read the Torah, Hebrew, and the fundamentals of Judaism.

Chesed - (Hebrew) Kindness.

Chevra Kadisha - (Aramaic) Jewish burial society composed of unpaid volunteers who provide funeral preparation for members of their congregations.

Cholent - (Yiddish) A traditional Jewish stew or baked dish, especially of meat, potatoes, beans, and barley; served on the Sabbath, but cooked the day before or overnight in a slow oven.

Chumash - (Hebrew) Pentateuch/The Five Books of Moses.

Chuppah - (Hebrew) Wedding canopy.

Churban - (Hebrew) Destruction.

Daven - (Yiddish) To pray.

Eem Yirtzeh Hashem - (Hebrew) G-d willing.

Erev - (Hebrew) Eve before *Shabbos* begins, or before a holiday begins.

Eynikl(ach) - /ay-nickel/- (Yiddish) grandchild/grandchildren.

Frum – (Yiddish) Religious.

Gan Eden - (Hebrew) Garden of Eden, heaven.

Gemara - (Aramaic) Another word for Talmud, which is the Oral Law passed down from G-d to Moses to the Jewish people. It eventually needed to be written down and was during the Babylonian exile in 586 BCE.

Gloypsi Gut - (Yiddish) Thank G-d.

Halacha - (Hebrew) Jewish law.

Handel - /hon-dle/ - (Yiddish) To bargain.

Hashem - (Hebrew) Literally "The Name," referring to G-d. We are not to pronounce His actual name casually, but only during prayers.

Havdalah - (Hebrew) 1) Separation. 2) A Jewish religious ceremony that marks the symbolic end of Shabbat and Jewish holidays and ushers in the new week.

Hesped - (Hebrew) Eulogy.

Istenem - (Hungarian) G-d.

Kaftan/Kapota - (Yiddish) Long black coat worn by Chassidic men.

Kaddish - (Hebrew) A liturgical prayer, recited at specified points during each of the three daily services and on certain other occasion such as by an individual who is in mourning for a deceased close relative for a period of eleven months

Kallah - (Hebrew) Bride.

Kaparos - (Hebrew) Asking for forgiveness from Hashem on the eve of Yom Kippur. Traditionally, this is accomplished by revolving a live chicken around one's own head. Symbolically, this represents that this animal's life should carry your sins and your life should be spared. Nowadays, it's become customary to take some amount of money, revolve this in place of the chicken, and give this money to charity as a symbol of repentance.

Kapo - (Italian) A prisoner in a Nazi concentration camp who was given food and privileges in return for supervising other prisoners doing forced labor; camp police.

Ketuba - (Hebrew) Jewish marriage contract.

Kibud av va-em - (Hebrew) Honoring your mother and father.

Kosher - (Hebrew) Following the dietary laws as set forth by G-d in the Torah.

Kriah - (Hebrew) To tear an article of clothing when a relative dies as an expression of mourning. For deceased parents you tear above the heart on the left; for other blood relatives, you tear on the right.

Levaya - (Hebrew) Funeral.

Matzah - (Hebrew) Unleavened bread eaten on the holiday of Passover.

Mechila - (Hebrew) Forgiveness.

Melamed - (Yiddush, Hebrew) Teacher.

Mensch - (Yiddish) Literally means a human being. It refers to a person of integrity and honor.

Mikvah - (Hebrew) A ritual bath in which Orthodox Jews are traditionally required to immerse on certain occasions, such as before the Sabbath and after each menstrual period to spiritually cleanse and purify themselves.

Minyan - (Hebrew) Quorum. A gathering of ten men is needed in order to pray as a group.

Mishna - (Hebrew) The first written recording of the Oral Torah of the Jewish people.

Mohel - (Hebrew) One who performs circumcision on a Jewish male as a religious rite.

Nachas - (Hebrew) Pride, joy.

Neni – (Hungarian) Aunt.

Niggun - (Hebrew) A tune or melody for a song.

Payess - (Yiddish) Sidecurls worn by Chassidic men.

Pesach - (Hebrew) Passover.

Potch - (Yiddish) A smack, slap or spank.

Purim - (Hebrew) A holiday dating back to 356 BCE. King Achashverosh (Ahaseuerus) of Babylonia had a wicked advisor, Haman who wished to destroy the Jewish population of the country. His plot was foiled and we celebrate our victory by dressing in costume, reading the history of this story [Megillat Esther], sending gifts of food to others, and donating charity to the poor.

Refuah Shlaima - (Hebrew) A quick and speedy recovery.

Ribono Shel Olam - (Hebrew) Master of the universe.

Rosh Hashana - (Hebrew) The Jewish New Year.

Sandek - (Hebrew) The man who holds the child during circumcision. It is the highest honor an individual can have within the ceremony.

Sefer Bereishis - (Hebrew) Genesis, the first of the five books of the Torah.

Shabbat/Shabbos - (Hebrew) Different pronunciations, but both mean "the day of rest." The Sabbath falls on Saturday.

Shabbaton - (Hebrew) Weekend retreat that takes place on *Shabbat*.

Shadchan - (Aramaic) Matchmaker.

Shaitel - (Yiddish) A wig. Its purpose is to cover the hair of a Jewish woman who is married as a form of modesty. Orthodox women usually wear a shaitel.

Shalosh Seudos - (Hebrew) The third meal on *Shabbos*.

Sheva Brachot - (Hebrew) Seven blessings. These are recited under the *chuppah*. There are also seven days of celebration following the wedding day where these same seven blessings are recited after the festive meal on each of those days.

Shiva - (Hebrew) A seven-day period of mourning.

Shiva Assar B'Tammuz - (Hebrew) The seventeenth of Tammuz.

Simcha - (Hebrew) Celebration.

Shloshim - (Hebrew) Completion of the first thirty-day period of mourning for the deceased by seven blood relatives: husband, wife, sister, brother, mother, father, and child.

Shoah - (Hebrew) Literally means "destruction." Term used to describe the Holocaust.

Shofar - (Hebrew) A ram's-horn trumpet used by ancient Jews in religious ceremonies and as a battle signal, now sounded at Rosh Hashana and Yom Kippur to usher in the New Year.

Shomer Shabbat - (Hebrew) A Sabbath observer.

Shtreimel - (Yiddish) Fur hat worn by many married Chassidic men on Shabbos, Jewish holidays, and other festive occasions.

Shul - (Yiddish) Synagogue.

Siddur - (Hebrew) Prayerbook.

Simchat Torah - (Hebrew) Rejoicing with the Torah. We complete the annual cycle of reading the last chapter in the Torah, and start reading from the beginning of the Torah again with Genesis. This takes place on the last day of Sukkot.

Skver Chassidim - (Yiddish) Sect of Chassidim that originated in Ukraine.

Sukkot - (Hebrew) Known as the Harvest holiday. For seven days we celebrate during autumn. Together we take the lulav (palm, willow, and myrtle branches) and the etrog (citron) and shake them in unison in a circular direction to demonstrate that Hashem is everywhere.

Tahara - (Hebrew) Traditional purification before the body is buried. It is washed in a ritual bath.

Tallis Ka-ton - (Hebrew) A small prayer shawl usually worn under a shirt, normally made of wool with special twined and knotted fringes called Tzi-tzit. These are attached to each of its four corners.

Talmud - (Hebrew) Oral Law passed down from G-d to Moses down to the Jewish people at Mount Sinai.

Tefillin - (Hebrew) Phylacteries.

Tehillim - (Hebrew) Psalms.

Tochter - (German, Yiddish) Daughter.

Torah - (Hebrew) Law. The commandments that the Jewish people received, given by G-d to Moses at Mount Sinai.

Tzadik - (Hebrew) Righteous person.

Tzedaka - (Hebrew) Charity.

Yad Vashem - (Hebrew) This is the name of the Holocaust museum in Jerusalem, Israel.

Yarmulke - (Yiddish) Head covering or skullcap that a Jewish man wears to show that G-d is above him at all times.

Yeshiva - (Hebrew) A Jewish private school.

Yiddish - Language originating in Germany between the thirteenth and fourteenth centuries which was spoken by the Jewish population. Incorporated into it were Hebrew words, German and Slavic influence. Yiddush is written with the Hebrew alphabet and therefore is read from right to left.

Yiddische mensch - (Yiddish) A very fine Jewish person.

Yiddishkeit - (Yiddish) Living the life of a Torah-observant Jew.

Yom Kippur - (Hebrew) Day of Atonement. The holiest day on the Jewish calendar, when we fast and ask for G-d's forgiveness, as well as that of our fellow man.

Yom Tov - (Hebrew) Literally means "Good Day." Expression of greeting to one another on holidays.

Yomim Tovim - (Hebrew) Plural of *Yom Tov*.

Zaidy - (Yiddish) Grandfather.

Zemiros - (Hebrew) Jewish songs or hymns set aside for the *Shabbos* and Jewish holiday table.

A NOTE ON PRONUNCIATION: The "Ch" in the Hebrew language has a guttural pronunciation. The "Ch" is pronounced as in "Bach", not as the "Ch" in "chair."

The ch will appear sometimes initially at the beginning of a word such as Challah. Other times in the middle of a word such as nachas or it will appear as the final sound such as in the word eyniklach.

APPENDIX

Towns and communities where my family lived before, during, and after the war:

Galszecs - Hungarian name for Sečovce, located in south-eastern Slovakia

Oborin - Slovakia

Svalyava - once was part of Czechoslovakia, now in western Ukraine

Király-Helmec – Hungary, now in Slovakia- Kralovsky Chlmec is name for town in Slovak

Miskolc - North-eastern Hungary

Holýšov - Czech Republic

Iloncza - Hungary

Michalovce - Eastern Slovakia

Kassa - Hungarian pronunciation for Košice, located in Slovakia

Nagyszöllös – Hungary/Czechoslovakia (today Ukraine)

FAMILY DOCUMENTS

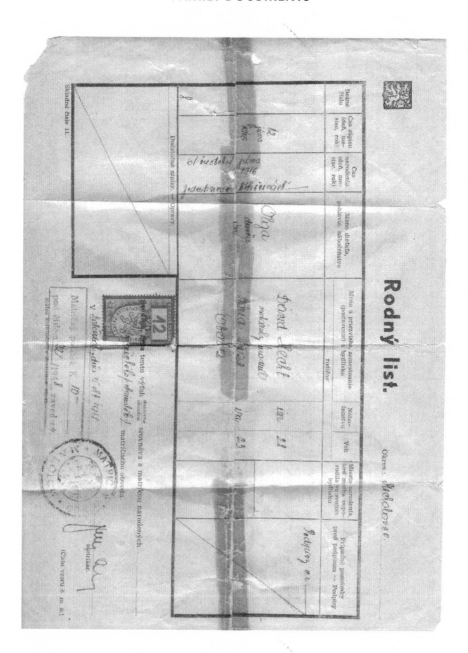

RODNY' LIST- BIRTH CERTIFICATE

Olga Gottesman's Birth Certificate

Birth certificate district: Michalovce

(Certificate divided into 9 columns)

1. Current number – 8
2. Date of record (day, month, year): Jun 12. 1916
3. Date of birth: Jun 6. 1916 (date wrote in words)
4. Name: Olga, girl, Jewish
5. Name and occupation of parents: David Hecht, notary clerk, Maria Prinz (Obor 12 – unknown referent)
6. Religion: Both Jewish
7. Age: David 28, Maria 23
8. Place of birth if not in place of permanent residency: [empty]
9. Notes: Signature

In Malčice, October 15. 1948, Signature of clerk

Fee: 10

Number: 78

507 900

```
H E C H T    Olga
verh.GOTTESMAN verw.STRAUSS
Elt.Dawid u.Margaret Printz
6.6.16          Oborin/CSR

4.44-   5.44  Gh-Ungwar
5.44-27.9.44  Auschwitz
9.44-   3.45  KL-Nuernberg
3.45- 5.5.45  KL-Holesin.CSR befr.

Ueber Polen u.Schweden n.USA

RBA f.Wg.Trier
f.RA.Levenson,Mue.                                    He.
```

Documentation obtained by the author from the United States Holocaust Memorial Museum in Washington, D.C. The Red Cross submitted this information to my family in order to receive restitution.

This states that Hecht, Olga (married Gottesman widowed Strauss)

Parents: David and Margaret Printz

Born 6.6.16   Oborin/Czechoslovakia

Dates of incarceration:

4.44- 5.44   Ghetto- Ungwar (Hungarian name for Uzhorod, today Ukraine)

5.44 - 27 .9.44   Auschwitz

9.44- 3.45 KL (Force Labor camp) Nuremberg, Germany

3.45- 5.5.45 KL (Force Labor camp) Holesin, Czechoslovakia

Went through Poland to Sweden and to the USA

Documentation obtained by the author from the United States Holocaust Memorial Museum in Washington, D.C. The date of birth 6.6.20 which is recorded here is incorrect. It was explained to the author that sometimes individuals wanted to appear older and sometimes to appear younger in order to live longer.

CC Prison Flossenburg, Nuremberg – Arrived October 18, 1944 from Auschwitz- On September 27, 1944, a selection at Auschwitz took place. This was the selection which brought a death sentence for Margit, Rozsi and Blanka Hecht: Olga's mother and two of her sisters. They were gassed three days later. After the selection Olga was moved from Barracks #31 to Barracks #28. Two weeks later she was transferred to the force labor camp of Nuremberg.

On March 16, 1945 Olga was transferred to Holleischen (Holýšov in Czechoslovakian) force labor camp.

The Germans had generated lists of women who were transferred to force labor camps, in this case, Holýšov. Individual cards were created by the Red Cross after the war from these lists in order to supply information to families about the fate of their loved ones. The Red Cross documents are part of the International Tracing Service.

ČESKOSLOVENSKÁ REPUBLIKA

Čís. adm. 583
5 / 194 6

„ evid.

Obec: B o Ľ
Okres: Královský Chlumec

27. marca 1946

Domovský list.

B o Ľ ..
.... potvrdzuje, že

........................Olga S t a v u a s v á rod. Chudík...

obyvateľ'(ka) v Sečovce , zamestnaním domáca

narodený(á) dňa 6.juna r. 1 ?16 v Oborin

stavu vydatá , má v tejto obci odo dňa narodenia

domovské právo

na zákl. §-u XXX 7 zákona č. XXII z roku 1386 a uzavretia

obecného zastupiteľ'stva zo dňa .... č. ..

Tento list vystavuje sa cieľom ako svedectvo

Boľu 25.mxxx februára 46
v_____ dňa_____194__

predn. obv úradu NV.

predseda NV.

Domovsky list

This document was issued on February 25 1946 in town Boľ (today Czech republic) in Kralovsky Chlumec county

It confirms that Olga Strausova born as Chechtova (this name is spelled incorrectly)

Has permanent residency in town Oborin (today Slovakia) since she was born.

Odpis:⁚⁚

Čis.adm.10.806-čis.evid.80/1948.Obec:Sečovce.Úrad
MNV:Sečovce.Okres: Trebišov.Dávka za úradný úkon
Kčs 15.-zaplatený pod pol.č.1267/1948.Nečitateľný
podpis v.r.---
12 Kčs kolok. Vysvedčenie o zachovalosti.Dočasná
miestna správna komisia v Sečovciach svedčí,že Ella
Reichová rod.Hecht 35 ročná /á/zamestnaním domáca
stavu vydatá,bytom v Sečovciach ulica Masaryková
čis.d.55,z ohľadu mravného bezvadne sa chová a do-
siaľ trestaný/á/ nebol/a/.-------------------------
Vysvedčenie toto bolo zhotovené na základe spoľah-
livého šetrenia o mravnej a osobnej spoľahlivosti
vyšemenovaného/ej/a môže byť použité k úradnej zá-
ležitosti.--
V Sečovciach dňa 27.októbra 1948.vedúci úradu MNV:
Karel v.r. Ú.P.Miľovčík v.r. predseda MNV.---------
Potvrdzujem,že Ella Reichová rod.Hechtová zo Sečo-
viec,okres Trebišov,je podľa tunajšej trestnej evi-
dencie po stránke mravnej zachovalá.-Sečovce 2.10.
1948.Ú.P.Veliteľ stanice štržm.Lučák - štržm.Lu-
čák v.r.--

Page 244

Odpis: crime registery

This document confirm that 35 years old Ella Reichova born as Hecht is married and lives in Sečovce on Masaryk street 55 has not committed any crime or moral lapse. It was issued and paid for in Sečovce on October 27. 1948.

Note to Reader: This type of document is necessary to receive a United States visa.

Matričný obvod Sečovce-okolie.

R o d n é   s v e d e c t v o.

Meno dieťaťa: E l l a ——————————————————————————————
Dátum narodenia a miesto narodenia: 20.dec.1913,Svaljava——
Rodičia: Dávid Hecht - Mária Princová ————————————————
Náboženstvo: izr. ——————————————————————————————

    Toto svedectvo vydávam na miesto rodného listu,ktorý ne-
možno zadovážiť na základe prevedeného šetrenia vypočutia hodno-
verných svedkov.-

    V Sečovciach dňa 13.novembra 1948.

                         Št.matrikár.

Rodne svedectvo: Birth certificate confirmation based on witnesses accounts. It was issued on 13. November 1948 in Sečovce.

Name of daughter : Ella born on December 20. 1913 in Svaljava (This is Ukraine today.)

Father: David Hecht

Mother Maria Princova both Jewish

Miestny národný výbor v D l h o m   K l č o v o m .

okres V r a n o v .

č. j. 1-50/1971.   dňa 6.novembra 1971.

P o t v r d e n i e .
‾‾‾‾‾‾‾‾‾‾‾‾‾‾‾‾‾‾‾‾‾

Rada miestneho národného výboru v Dlhom Klčovom,okres Vranov n/T
na základe dolupodpísaných svedkov,týmto potvrdzuje,že za tzv.
slovenského štátu dňa 3.5.1942 a 7.5.1942 boli Isadorovi Reichovi
bytom t.č.181 Brighten Ave Perth Amboy N.Y.08861 USA deportovaní
rodičia a súrodenci do koncentračných táborov,kde sa doposiaľ
nevrátili.Doleuvedení mali trvalé bydlisko v tun.obci,a to:
    1./ Markus /Elias / Reich ,otec
    2./ Rosalia Reichová,matka
    3./ Aron Reich, brat
    4./ Dezider / Tobias/Reich,brat
    5./ Samuel Reich, brat
    6./ Victor Reich,brat
    7./ Margita Reichová ,sestra
    Toto potvrdenie vydáva sa pre úradnú potrebu a hodnovernosť
uvedeného potvrdzujú svedkovia.

1/ Dzurevčín Jura
2/ Dzura Michal

Predsede MNV:

Issued on November 6 1971 in Dlhé Klčkovo which is in Vranov Nad
Topľou County.

City Hall committee confirms that parents and siblings of Isadore Reich who lives 181 Brighton Ave Perth Amboy NY 08861 USA were deported during Slovak State in period from 5.3.1942 to 5.7. 1942 from Dlhé Klčkovo to concentration camps and never came back.

List:

1. Markus (Elias) Reich, father
2. Rosalia Reich, mother
3. Aron Reich, brother
4. Dezider (Tobias) Reich, brother
5. Samuel Reich, brother
6. Victor Reich, brother
7. Margarita Reich, sister

This is confirmed by reliable witness accounts.

5708/1746.

Jakub Izidor   R e i ch.

Obchodník

1.júna 1909,

Kvakovce okres Vranov.

Kvakovce   Vranov

Sečovciach

Ella   Hechtová   20.decembra

1913   Svalave   Svalava

x

x

x

x

Trebišove   2.aprila 1946.

Certificate of Czechoslovakia citizenship for Jakub Izidor Reich. Occupation merchant. Born on June 1. 1909 in Kvakovce which is Vranov nad Topľou county. Residency in Sečovce.

His wife has also Czechoslovak citizenship.

Ella Hecht born on December 20. 1913 in Svaljava. No kids.

Document was issued in Trebišov on April 2. 1946.

Odpis:...

1/2

12 05

8. 11. 1948.

crime registery

This document confirms that 39 years old Jakub Izidor Reich lives in Sečovce on Masaryk Street 184 is married and has not committed any crime or moral lapse. It was issued and paid for in Sečovce on November 8. 1948.

Note to Reader: This type of document is necessary to receive a United States visa.

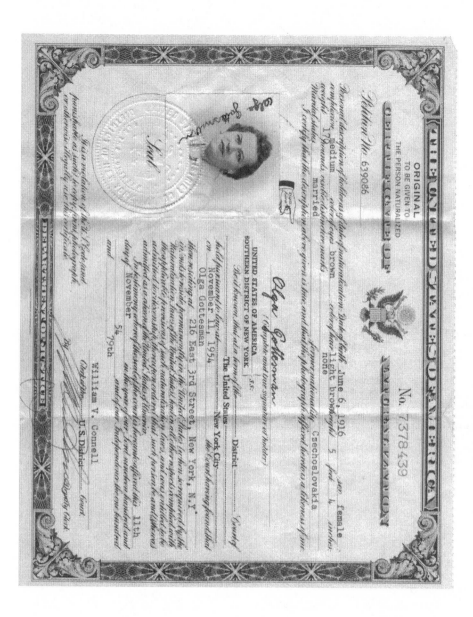

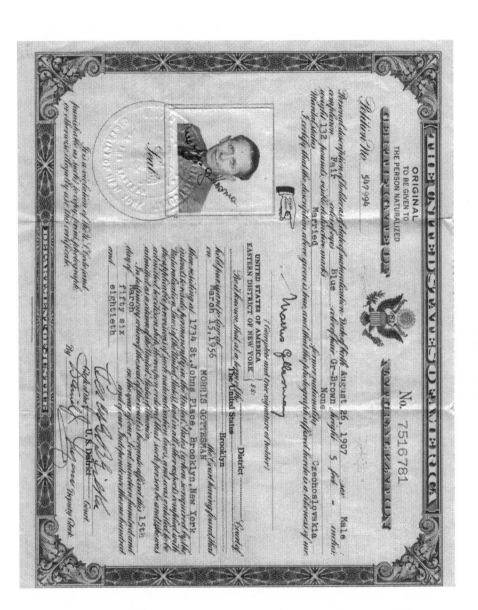

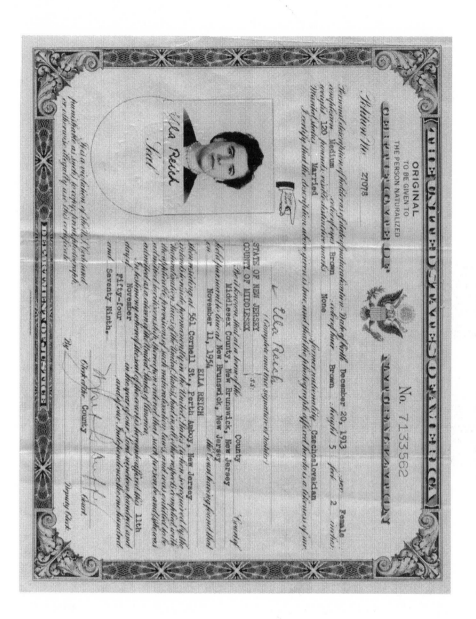

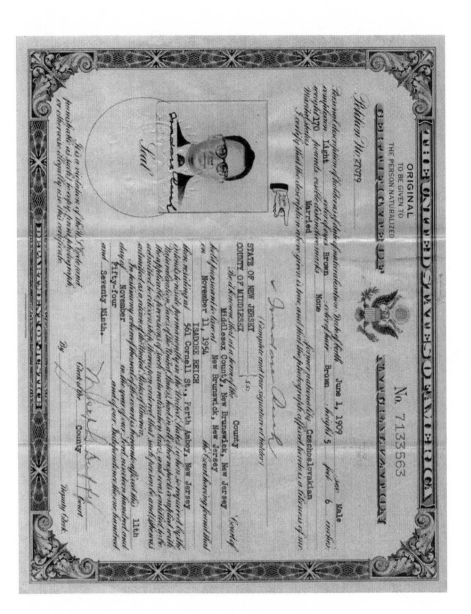

My grandparents' engagement announcement:

Margit Princz   David Hecht

Engaged

Szilvasujfalu   Abara

In February 1912

Aunt Ella and Uncle Isadore's wedding invitation:

בס"ד

WIR LADEN SIE HÖFL. ZUR TRAUUNG UNSERER
KINDER

ELLA UND ISIDOR

WELCHE AM 20. AUGUST (כא אב) UM 4 UHR NACH-
MITTAGS IN OBORIN STATTFINDEN WIRD.

OBORIN   AUGUST 1935   KOLČ.-DLUHE

DAVID HECHT   ELIAS REICH
& FRAU   & FRAU

DINER 6 UHR

TELEGRAMME: HECHT OBORIN MALČICE.

GLOBUS SEČOVCE

We invite you to the wedding of our
children

Ella and Isidor

Which will take place on August 20 (21 Av) at 4 O'clock in the
afternoon
in Oborin

Oborin August 1935   Kolč-Dluhe

David Hecht   Elias Reich
and wife   and wife

Dinner at 6 O'clock

Telegram: Hecht Oborin Malčice

Globus Sečovce
(Name of Telegram company)

Letter of Response from David Hecht to Margit Princz- 1912

Translation

My dearest little woman, Margit, With joy I wanted them. They were exceptionally good, but am I angry at you? How could I be? Not for the whole world. The only thing I can write (maybe it is not news because it is Friday) is that they fry cheese dough, which is very good.

Regards from your faithful and devoted, Hecht

Your Honor
Princz Margitka (Margaret)
For the Young Lady

Szilvás Ŭjfalŭ
12 Kozma
Austro-Hungary

Goldenberg and Hecht Publication, Szolyva (Svalyava), Reproduction prohibited

In the Jewish tradition, every baby born receives a Hebrew name. Some parents choose to give a popular name as well, according to their nationality or taste.

On the Hecht side, I have put the given name first, then the Hebrew name and date of birth. Parents are listed first:

David (Dovid, 1888; died in Auschwitz, Dec. 1944)

Margit (Miriam, 1892; died in Auschwitz, Sept. 1944)

1. Ella (Esther, December 20, 1913; died June 2011)
2. Olga (Rivka, June 6, 1916; died June 1988)
3. Ernő, (Yitzchak, July 6, 1918; died in Auschwitz, Dec. 1944)
4. Roze, nicknamed Rozsika, (Rochel Leah, August 4, 1921; died in Auschwitz, Sept. 1944)
5. Blanka, nicknamed Blanki, (Devora, September 4, 1924; died in Auschwitz, Sept. 1944)
6. Zoltan, nicknamed Zolika (Avrahom Dov, February 28, 1929; died in Auschwitz, Dec.1944)

On the Gottesman side, I put the Hebrew names first, then the given names. I only have knowledge of some of their birthdates and dates of death. Parents are listed first:

Shaya (Yishayahu, 1868; died in Auschwitz, 1942)

Fani (Freida, 1869; died in Auschwitz, 1942)

1. Yitzchak (Missing in action, assumed in Italy, 1915)
2. Yisrael (Died in Auschwitz concentration camp 1942)
3. Sora (Sara, died in Auschwitz concentration camp 1942)
4. Rochel (Roncze, born 1901; died of infantile enteritis (inflammation of the small intestine), July 18, 1904)
5. *Pearl (Gyongyi, born April 29,1902; died of inflammation of the lung, July 2, 1912)
6. Avrahom Moshe (Abraham Mozes, nicknamed Avrahom Moishku, born August 26, 1907; died of congestive heart failure, October 25, 2003)
7. Arieh Lieb (nicknamed Lieby, born March, 1909; died October 8, 1985)
8. *Leah (Lenke, born 1912; died of inflammation of the lung, March 19, 1918)
9. *Nosson (Nathan, born 1914; died of inflammation of the lung, October 13, 1918)

*Inflammation of the lung could refer to pneumonia causing influenza which is what my father said was the cause of their deaths.

ADDITIONAL FAMILY PHOTOS

Aleksander Hecht, 1922

Margit Princz Hecht, early 1900s

Blanka, Zoli and Rozsi Hecht, mid 1930s

Rozsi, David, Zoli, Margit and Olga, ~1940

Ella Hecht Reich, 1915

Blanka Hecht, friend,
Rozsi Hecht, 1942-43

Fani Gottesman (right) Morris's mother, Sara (oldest sister to Morris Gottesman) ~1920s

Isadore Reich (rear left) and family, ~1922

Miriam at Auschwitz / Birkenau, Barrack 31 – where her grandmother, mother, and aunts were imprisoned.

Yaakov and Miriam's wedding, 1986

Rivki, Uncle Isadore Reich, Dovid, Aunt Ella Reich, baby Asher (1991)

Dovid, Rivki and Asher Dobin (Purim, 1994)

Hugo Princz, Magda and Hershey Gottesman, Asher Dobin, Morris Gottesman, Yaakov, Rivki, Miriam (Gottesman) and Dovid Dobin at Morris's 89th Birthday Party, 1996.

Morris with grandson, Dovid, at Dovid's Bar-Mitzvah

Rivki with Grandfather, Morris

Asher with Aunt Ella at his Bar-Mitzvah

Asher's college graduation

About the Author

Miriam Dobin is married with three children and has worked as an Early Childhood educator for over 20 years. She graduated Yeshiva University Stern College for Women with a degree in Education and received her certification as Teacher of the Handicapped from Kean University. She is a licensed teacher in the State of New Jersey. Miriam currently serves as the Head Teacher in the Early Childhood division of a local school. Miriam has taught Holocaust studies to middle school students and is deeply committed to furthering knowledge of this period in history.

Upon the death of her beloved aunt, Miriam promised herself that the time had come to write the family history. Her task took her deep into the family records and half way around the world to the places where her parents, grandparents, aunts, uncles and cousins lived before they were imprisoned in Nazi concentration camps and where almost all of them were killed. Miriam was raised not only by her two parents but also by her aunt and uncle, all four of them survivors. Together these four individuals reared a child who, for them, embodied a future that they could hardly have believed would ever come. Miriam's life is a living legacy to the strength and perseverance of these four individuals, who together instilled in Miriam a strong sense of responsibility and commitment to Jewish life, family and continuity.